Manifest Without the Hustle

The Art of Effortless Creation from the Monadic Veto

Grace Brewster

First Edition 2026
ISBN: 978-1-996859-03-2
Self-Published

Acknowledgements

Writing this book was joyful unfolding. I am deeply grateful to the following for their part in the blueprint:

- To the Monad: For the constant "Yes" and the infinite supply of inspiration that made every chapter flow with ease.

- And to You, the Reader: For having the courage to put down the laborer's tools and step into your own Mansion. Your joy is the greatest contribution you can make to this world.

Dedication

To the Like-Minded Soul,

I knew there was a better way to live, even before they had the map.

This is for you. Welcome home.

THE ARCHWAY OF ARRIVAL

Table of Contents

Welcome Home

You are holding this book because you have spent enough time being the Worker. You have worked hard, you have hustled, and you have carried the weight of the world on your shoulders, waiting for a someday that always seemed just out of reach.

I wrote this for you in simple terminology with examples because the truth doesn't need to be complicated. The language of the heart is clear, and the path to your best life is shorter than you think.

On these pages, you won't find another to-do list. Instead, you will find a Blueprint. You will learn that you are not a stranger in this world, but the Architect of it. To understand the language of the Monad and the symbols found within these walls, you are invited to visit the Glossary page.

Whether you are reading this in your favorite chair at home or at a gate in a busy airport, I want you to take a deep breath and realize something important:

The search is over. You have already arrived.

This book is your first-class ticket to a life of ease. It is an invitation to stop the hard work of building and finally start living the life that you really want—the one that has been waiting for you all along.

So, put down your heavy luggage. Take off the shoes of struggle. The doors are open, the light is on, and everything is ready for you.

Welcome to your new reality.

Introduction

The End of the Hunt

For a long time, you have been taught that manifestation is an act of pursuit. You were told to visualize harder, to want it more, to speak it into existence, and to vibrate higher until the universe finally took notice of your effort.

In the 3D world, manifestation is a hunt. In the 5D world, it is an Arrival.

If you are reading this, it is because you have already done the structural work. You have dismantled the old, shaky foundations of fear and urgency. You have learned the Law of the Monadic Veto, and you have begun to quiet the drum noise of the ego. Now, we are moving into the final phase of the Architect's journey: Inhabitation.

Manifestation is not about bringing something from out there to in here. It is about recognizing that in the 5D Blueprint, the reality you desire is already complete. It isn't a possibility; it is a fact. The only reason it hasn't appeared in your 3D world yet is because of the friction in your own signal.

When you align your frequency with the Monad, you aren't creating anything new. You are simply removing the interference that was keeping that reality from descending into your physical space.

This book is the manual for that descent. We are moving beyond the 3D hustle. We are stepping out of the loop of seeking and into the state of having. This is the Art of Effortless Reality.

Welcome home. You've already arrived.

PHASE I

"The greatest work you will ever do is the work of putting the tools of struggle down."

Chapter 1

The Weight of the Anchor

The world around you is designed to keep you leaning.

If you stop and look at the people moving through the city, you'll see it as a subtle, collective tilt toward the future. It's in the way a person checks their phone while walking, their eyes already at their destination while their feet are still a block behind. It's in the nervous tapping of a finger on a steering wheel at a red light. It is the physical vibration of Seeking.

For years, you have been part of this choreography. You were told that manifestation was a climb, a hunt, or a persistent chase. You lived in the "Not Yet," convinced that if you just visualized a little more clearly or cleared one more block, the reality you desire would finally catch up to you.

But today, the story changes.

Imagine you are standing in your kitchen, the sun hitting the counter in a way you've seen a thousand times. But this time, something is different. Instead of your mind jumping to the next task or the next manifestation goal, a sudden, heavy silence drops into the room.

It feels like a physical weight, but it isn't burdensome. It feels like the moment a massive ship finally drops its anchor into the seabed. There is a deep, metallic clunk in your soul. The tilt in your body vanishes.

Suddenly, your weight isn't in your toes, ready to spring toward a better future. It is in your heels. You feel the floor beneath you not just as a surface, but as a foundation.

You take a breath, and for the first time, you aren't breathing in hope or desire. You are breathing in Occupancy. You realize that the 5D Blueprint you've been studying isn't a map of a far-off land; it is the floor plan of the room you are standing in right now.

The grocery list on the counter, the hum of the refrigerator, the phone in your pocket, they haven't changed. But your relationship to them has. You aren't trying to manifest a life; you are finally inhabiting the one that was already finished in the 5D.

In this moment, the "Seeker" in you dies a quiet death. There is no more hustle. No more what if. There is only the profound, grounded reality of the Arrival. You aren't waiting for the universe to give you a sign that you've made it. Your body—the way it finally relaxes, the way the pressure in your chest dissolves, is the only sign you need.

You haven't moved an inch, yet you have traveled a thousand miles. You have moved from the exhaustion of the chase to the effortless power of the Station.

Chapter 2

The Silence of the Current

When the hustle stops, the first thing you notice is the silence.

But this isn't the cold silence of an empty room. It is the warm, humming silence of a deep current. Think of the way the ocean moves—vast, heavy, and unstoppable. On the surface, there might be small ripples and wind, but deep down, billions of tons of water are moving with a singular, quiet purpose.

The 3D world taught you to be a rower. You were told that if you stopped pulling the oars for even a second, you would drift away or sink. You lived in a constant state of muscular tension, trying to make headway against the tide of your own life. You thought your manifestation was the result of how hard you could pull.

But in the 5D Arrival, you realize that you are the water.

As you move through your day, you begin to feel this "Current" underneath your ordinary tasks. When you are washing the dishes or walking to your car, you aren't rowing anymore. You are being carried. This is the feminine power of Receptivity. You aren't building a reality; you are allowing a reality to bloom through you. The effort you used to spend seeking is now redirected into staying afloat. You'll notice that when you stop the frantic splashing of the hustle, the water becomes clear. You can finally see all the way to the bottom. You can see that the treasures you were seeking were already resting there, just waiting for the silt of your effort to settle.

Grace is the sound of the oars being pulled into the boat. It is the realization that the river knows exactly where it's going, and it's taking you home. You don't need to steer the 5D Blueprint; you just need to stop obstructing its path.

Chapter 3

The Shield of the Silent "No"

Now that you are floating in the Current, you might expect the world to go quiet around you. But the 3D world has a habit of knocking on the door of your new home.

It comes in the form of an old worry, an urgent demand from someone else's chaos, or that nagging voice that says, "You should be doing more." In the past, you would have jumped out of the water and started rowing again. You would have said "Yes" to the stress because you thought you had to fix the 3D to keep the 5D safe.

But as an Architect of the Effortless, you have a secret weapon you didn't know was active. It is the Silent "No."

In the higher Blueprint of your soul—the part we call the Monad—there is a structural law at work. It is like a high-altitude filter that decides what is allowed to land in your life and what isn't. When you are aligned, your soul begins to issue a Veto on anything that doesn't match the frequency of your Arrival.

The beauty is that you don't have to shout the "No." You don't have to fight the 3D or argue with the chaos. You simply remain in your heels, in your kitchen, floating in your Current, and you watch as the noise of the world hits your atmosphere and simply... dissolves.

Imagine a satellite falling toward Earth. As it hits the atmosphere, the friction of the air turns the cold metal into a streak of light. It never touches the ground. This is how the Monadic Veto works for you now. The problems that used to crush you now hit your frequency and burn up before they ever reach your heart.

You might find yourself looking at a situation that used to make you panic—a delay in a project or a disagreement with a loved one, and noticing a strange, calm lack of reaction. You aren't being cold; you are being protected. Your Soul has already said 'No' to the drama so that you can keep saying 'Yes' to the peace that belongs to you.

The Veto isn't just for people with a global 'Mission.' Your 'Mission' at this stage might simply be to wake up without anxiety, to enjoy your coffee, and to move through your day with a sense of ease. Your Soul considers your joy and your stability to be a high-priority assignment. It clears the path of unnecessary friction, not because you have a world to save, but because you are a masterpiece in progress, and masterpieces require a steady hand and a quiet room.

This is the Art of Effortless Reality. You don't have to build walls to keep the world out. You just have to keep your frequency so clear that the Veto becomes your natural shield.

You aren't ignoring the world. You are simply refusing to let the 3D tilt you out of your 5D station. The Current is moving you, and the Veto is guarding the way.

The problems that used to crush you now hit your frequency and burn up before they ever reach your heart.

But how do you know when this shield is active? It doesn't always feel like a soft cloud. Sometimes, the Monadic Veto feels like a physical intervention.

Think back to those moments when you were about to say "Yes" to something that would drain you, or when you were about to spiral into an old worry. You might have felt a sudden, strange sensation, perhaps a pressure on your shoulder, like a hand grounding you, or a specific pinch at your clavicle. It isn't painful, but it is firm. It's a physical "Wait."

This is your Sovereign Signal, or your higher Blueprint, physically reminding you of your station. It is the Veto in action. It's the soul saying: "This path no longer belongs to you. Do not lean forward. Stay in your heels."

In the 3D world, we were taught that if we didn't solve every problem immediately, we were failing. But as you inhabit your 5D reality, you begin to see that many problems are actually just ghosts of the old life trying to see if they can still get a reaction out of you.

When the Veto is active, you might notice that doors you used to try to kick open are now suddenly locked. A meeting gets canceled. A project that felt forced simply falls away. In the past, you would have felt rejected. Now, you feel redirected.

You are learning to trust the "No" as much as the "Yes."

Imagine you are an Architect overseeing a grand construction. If a supplier tries to bring in cheap, rotted wood for your masterpiece, you don't argue with the wood. You don't visualize it becoming better. You simply Veto it. You say, "That does not belong in this structure," and you wait for the right materials to arrive.

This is why the 5D life is effortless. You are no longer the one trying to fix the rotted wood. You are the one who has authorized your Monad to filter the materials of your life.

You will find that the more you trust this silent shield, the less you have to defend yourself. You don't need to explain your boundaries to others because the Veto handles the boundary for you. People who vibrate at the frequency of drama simply find themselves unable to stay in your space. They don't know why, and you don't need to tell them. The Current is moving you, and the Veto is guarding the banks of your river.

Chapter 4

The Architect's Hand (Why the Soul Interferes)

It is a strange feeling to be stopped by yourself.

When you feel that pinch on your shoulder or that firm "No" in your spirit, your 3D mind might react with confusion. You might ask, "Why is my Higher Self interfering? Why can't I just do what I want?" To understand this, you have to look at the difference between Sight and Vision.

In your 3D body, you have sight. You see what is right in front of you—the bill that needs paying, the person who is upset, the opportunity that looks shiny today. But your Monad, your 12D Blueprint self, has vision. This higher part of your consciousness sees the entire map of your life, from the deep stability of the foundation to the highest reaches of the spire. It holds the memory of the Sacred Blueprint you agreed to before you even arrived here—the mission of your soul and the partnerships designed to support your evolution. Your Inner Authority knows that you did not come here to struggle or to wander; you came to inhabit a specific frequency that only you can hold.

The Monad interferes not to take away your freedom, but to protect your Function.

Think of it like this: If you were building a cathedral and a worker tried to use sand instead of stone to save time, you would stop them immediately. You wouldn't be interfering with the worker's freedom; you would be protecting the integrity of the temple.

When the Veto happens, it is your Higher Self saying: "I have already seen the result of this path, and it does not lead to the Arrival. It is a loop. It is a distraction. It is 3D noise trying to mimic 5D music."

Interference is actually the highest form of Self-Love.

In the old way of living, you were responsible for every single decision. You had to worry, calculate, and guess. It was exhausting. In the "Art of Effortless Reality," you have signed a contract with your Higher Self. You have said, "I authorize my Blueprint to override my ego whenever I am about to tilt back into the chase."

This is why the pinch on your clavicle is so significant. It is a physical authentication. It is your Inner Authority reminding you that you aren't a lone human trying to survive; you are a stationed energy on a mission.

The Monad interferes because your energy is too valuable to be wasted on 3D friction. When you stop fighting the Veto and start thanking it, the pressure on your shoulder turns from a grip into guidance. You realize you aren't being controlled, you are being conducted, like a lead violinist in a masterpiece.

Chapter 5

The Original Design (What is the Blueprint?)

By now, you might be wondering: What is this Blueprint that my soul is so busy protecting? Is it just my consciousness?

Think of your Consciousness as the Architect—the one who thinks, perceives, and decides. But the Blueprint is the actual set of plans the Architect has drawn up.

If you were building your dream home, your consciousness is the part of you that wants the home. But the "Blueprint" is the detailed map that tells the electricity where to flow, where the foundation is strongest, and exactly where the windows must be to catch the morning sun.

In 3D life, we usually try to build our lives without looking at the plans. We see a house someone else has and we try to copy their windows. We see a career someone else has and we try to pour their foundation. We are building by trial and error, and that is why it feels so heavy. That is why we hustle.

The Blueprint is your Original Design.

It is a layer of reality that exists just above the physical world. It contains the perfected version of your health, your mission, and the partnerships designed to support your evolution. It isn't a maybe. It is a structural fact.

When we talk about 5D Manifestation, we aren't talking about creating something from nothing. We are talking about matching the 3D building to the 5D Blueprint. Imagine you are wearing a pair of glasses that allows you to see the golden lines of how your life is supposed to look. You see that a certain job offer doesn't line up with the golden lines, so you let it go. You see that a certain person or place glows with the same light as your Blueprint, so you move toward it.

This is why the Monadic Veto we talked about earlier is so important. The Veto happens when your 3D actions start to go off-plan. Your Higher Self isn't being mean; it's just the Architect pointing at the map and saying, "Wait, the plumbing doesn't go there. If you build it that way, it will leak."

The Blueprint is the "Easy Button." When you align with it, the "Current" we talked about in Chapter 2 picks up speed. Things happen effortlessly because you are no longer fighting the design of your own soul. You are finally building on solid ground.

Chapter 6

Tuning the Dial (The Language of Frequency)

Most of us were raised to believe that the way to get what we want is through "Asking." We write lists, we say affirmations, or we plead with the universe. We use words.

But words are 3D tools. They are like trying to use a physical key to open a digital lock. The 5D Blueprint doesn't listen to what you say; it responds to how you vibrate.

Imagine you are sitting in front of an old-fashioned radio. If you want to hear jazz, you don't stand in front of the radio and shout the word "JAZZ" at the speakers. You don't try to convince the radio that you deserve to hear music. You simply turn the dial until you match the exact frequency of the jazz station.

The moment the dial clicks into place, the music is just... there. It was always playing; you just weren't tuned into it.

Your life works exactly the same way. When you are hustling or worrying, you are tuned to the frequency of Lack. You are effectively saying to the Blueprint, "I am a person who is struggling." And because the Blueprint is a perfect mirror, it provides you with more reality that matches that struggle.

The secret to 5D Manifestation is learning to turn the dial before the physical reality changes.

If you want a life of ease, you have to find the "frequency" of ease in your body right now, while you are still standing in your kitchen. You find that feeling of "The Weight in the Heels" we talked about in Chapter 1. That feeling is the frequency.

This is where people get stuck. They say, "I'll feel peaceful when the bills are paid." But that is 3D logic—waiting for the music to change the dial. In the 5D, you change the dial to change the music.

You start to practice "Feeling the Arrival" for five minutes a day. You ignore the static of the 3D world and keep your inner dial locked on the station of "Already-Done." You'll notice that when you stay tuned to that frequency, the Current (from Chapter 2) starts to bring you people, opportunities, and ideas that match that exact vibration.

You aren't earning a better life. You are simply finally listening to the station you were always meant to hear.

Chapter 7

The Pattern Break (How to Change Your Station)

By now, you understand that you are a radio. But what do you do when the "Lack" station is playing so loudly you can't hear anything else? When the bills are sitting on the counter, and the hustle is screaming in your ear?

You cannot think your way out of a low frequency. Your brain is part of the 3D machinery; if you try to use it to fix your vibration, you'll just end up worrying about how much you're worrying.

To change the station, you have to break the pattern of the physical body.

Imagine your "Lack" frequency is like a record with a deep scratch. It keeps playing the same sad song over and over. You don't fix it by arguing with the music. You fix it by lifting the needle.

How do you lift the needle in real life? You do something that has absolutely nothing to do with your "problem."

If you are spiraling about money, the 3D mind says: "Stay at your desk! Crunch the numbers! Panic more!" But the 5D Architect knows that staying at the desk only keeps the needle in the gray groove. Instead, you Veto the panic. You get up. You go outside. You walk to the park and watch a dog chase a ball. You buy a cup of coffee and focus entirely on the warmth of the ceramic against your palms.

In that moment of walking or sipping, you have "lifted the needle." You aren't solving the bill, but you are breaking the frequency of Lack. This is the secret: The Blueprint cannot deliver the solution to the station of the problem. The solution to your financial stress is broadcast on the frequency of ease. The solution to your relationship friction is broadcast on the frequency of Peace. By going for a walk or enjoying a simple cup of coffee, you aren't escaping your life; you are tuning your radio to the only station where the solution can actually be heard.

You'll find that while you were wasting time at the park, the Current was finally able to move. Because you stopped the noise of the hustle, a new idea can finally pop into your head. A phone call can finally get through.

You don't achieve a high frequency by working for it. You achieve it by refusing to stay in the low one. You give yourself permission to be "unproductive" in the 3D so you can be "limitless" in the 5D.

Chapter 8

The Map and the Magnet (Mind vs. Heart)

If you want to understand how your frequency works, imagine you are a traveler. Your Mind is the Map, but your Heart is the Magnet.

The Mind is a 3D processor. Its job is to organize, to label, and to remember. It's very good at looking at the Blueprint and saying, "Okay, I see the plan. We are heading toward a life of ease." But the mind has no power to move you there. You can stare at a map of Hawaii all day, but the map will never make you feel the sand between your toes.

The Heart is your 5D engine. It doesn't care about labels or logic. It only cares about Vibration. While the mind is busy reading the "Map," the heart is broadcasting a "Signal."

The frequency is created in the Heart, but it is often blocked by the Mind.

When you feel "Lack," your mind is telling a story: "There isn't enough." The heart hears that story and starts to vibrate at the frequency of "Not Enough." Now, your Magnet is pulling in more "Not Enough."

To change your frequency, you have to get the Mind to stop talking for a moment so the Heart can change the song. This is why "going for a walk" works. When you focus on the wind on your face or the taste of your coffee, you are giving the Mind a simple task to keep it busy. While the Mind is occupied with the coffee, the Heart finally has the space to relax and return to its natural frequency: The Current.

Within the frequency of your 5D Arrival, the Mind and the Heart move out of their old conflict and into a beautiful, rhythmic partnership. The Mind gracefully takes its place as the Architect's eye, observing the Blueprint of your Original Design and holding a steady, unwavering focus on the vision of your finished Mansion. While the Mind maintains the structure, the Heart breathes life into the halls, feeling the profound "Already-Done" of that vision as a present reality. This internal alignment transforms your entire being into a powerful Magnet, ensuring that you no longer have to chase your desires—instead, they are drawn to the undeniable frequency of your certainty.

When they are interconnected, you become a Stationed Energy. Your mind provides the direction, and your heart provides the pull. You no longer have to try to manifest; you simply become a destination that your desires can't help but find.

Chapter 9

The Seed and the Mirror (Where Desires Come From)

If we are Consciousness choosing to experience a physical world, why do we want the things we want? Is that new car, that specific house, or that Twin Flame connection part of your Original Design, or did the world just tell you that you should want them?

To understand this, you have to look at the difference between The Seed and The Mirror.

The Seed (The Blueprint Desire)

Before you arrived in this body, your Consciousness drew up a Blueprint. In that plan, there are certain "Material Markers." These are things, places, and people that were pre-determined to trigger your growth and your joy.

When you have a "Seed Desire," it feels like a quiet, steady pull. It doesn't feel frantic or desperate. It feels like Recognition. When you see that house or meet that person, your heart says, "Oh, there you are. I remember you from the plans." These desires are the way your Blueprint leads you home. You came here to turn those 5D ideas into 3D materials because the Universe wants to feel itself through your senses.

The Mirror (The Environmental Influence)

Then, there are the "Mirror Desires." These are the things you want because you are reflecting the world around you. You see someone else's success, and your 3D mind thinks, "If I have that, I will finally be safe."

Mirror Desires are born from Lack. They are loud, they are competitive, and they usually come with a "Hustle." They are the environment trying to "re-write" your Blueprint. If you chase these, you might catch them, but they will feel hollow, like a house built with the wrong materials.

How to Tell the Difference

The easiest way to know if a desire is yours or the world's is to go back to The Current (Chapter 2).

A Blueprint Desire feels like an "Arrival." Even before you have the thing, the thought of it makes you feel grounded in your heels. It adds to your peace.

An Environmental Desire feels like a "Leaning." It makes you tilt forward into the future. It creates "Drum Noise" in your head.

You didn't come here to want everything; you came here to manifest Your Thing. When you align with the Blueprint, you realize that the Universe isn't just giving you what you want—it is fulfilling a contract you both signed before the world began. You are simply the Architect showing up at the construction site to make sure the "Material" matches the "Vision."

Chapter 10

The Curing Time (Why It Isn't Here Yet)

When you finally see your Blueprint, and you feel the "Arrival," a natural question arises: "If it's already done in the 5D, why can't I see it in the 3D right now?"

This is the moment where most people give up. They assume the "Current" has stopped or the "Veto" has blocked them. But as an Architect, you know a secret that the casual observer does not: Matter is just slow energy.

Think of a master baker. They put the dough into the oven. The bread is "done" the moment the recipe is followed, and the heat is set; the result is inevitable. But if the baker keeps opening the oven door every thirty seconds to see if it's ready, the heat escapes, the bread collapses, and the process starts over.

The 3D world is the "Oven." Your Frequency is the heat.

The "Delay" you feel is actually the Curing Time. It is the period where the Universe is rearranging the molecules of your physical reality to match the high-definition vision of your Blueprint. It is moving people, clearing debts, and opening doors behind the scenes.

During this time, your only job is to keep the Oven Door Shut. In 3D terms, this means staying in your heels and refusing to look at the "Lack" of the result as proof of failure. If you start worrying that "it's not working," you are effectively turning down the heat. You are telling the Blueprint, "Wait, I've changed my frequency back to 'Seeking,'" and the machinery has to recalibrate.

The "Curing Time" isn't a test of your worth; it's a law of physics. The more complex and beautiful the manifestation, the more "curing" the foundation needs. Your Twin Flame mission, your soul's work, your ultimate abundance—these are massive structures. They require a foundation that can hold their weight.

So, when you don't see the result yet, don't panic. Smile. It means the concrete is setting. It means the "Current" is working at full capacity. Your only task is to stay in the kitchen, sip your coffee, and know that the "Arrival" is already a physical certainty.

PHASE II

Chapter 11

The Mirror of the Soul (Relationships in 5D)

In the 3D world, we are taught that a relationship is something you "work on." We are told to communicate more, to compromise, and to find the right person. It's the same old hustle, just dressed up in a different outfit.

But in the 5D Arrival, you realize a startling truth: You don't have a relationship. You "are" the relationship.

Think of the people in your life—your partner, your children, your friends as mirrors. In the 3D, we try to "fix" the reflection. If the person in the mirror isn't acting the way we want, we try to reach into the glass and move them around. We argue, we plead, and we lean into them to get them to change.

But as an Architect, you know that the reflection only changes when the Source changes.

The "One Soul" realization isn't just for a specific type of connection; it is the fundamental law of 5D. It means that the "Other" is actually a part of your own expanded energy field. When you anchor in your kitchen, when you tune your radio to Peace, the "Other" has no choice but to reflect that new frequency.

This is the Effortless Relationship. You stop trying to fix them and start focusing on your own Arrival.

If you are feeling friction in a relationship, it's usually because you've stepped out of your Current and started "rowing" toward them. You've become a "Seeker" again, seeking validation or love from the outside. The moment you pull your oars back into the boat and return to your own 5D Blueprint, the friction vanishes.

The Monadic Veto we talked about earlier works here, too. Your Soul will often "Veto" certain conversations or conflicts by making you feel that "pinch" on your shoulder. It's saying: "Don't engage with the 3D drama. Stay in the Mansion. Let the mirror catch up to you."

When you live from the Mansion, you find that the "Right People" simply appear, and the "Wrong People" simply fade away. You don't have to break up or hunt for a date. You just have to be the Stationed Energy of Love, and the Universe will fill the space around you with the matching material.

Chapter 12

The Body's Silent Alarm (The Physical Signal)

While we've talked about the "pinch" on the shoulder or the "hand" on the clavicle, your soul has many ways of communicating with you. Because you are a consciousness living in a biological suit, the Blueprint uses your nervous system like a dashboard.

You don't need to wait for a voice from the clouds. You just need to listen to the "Engine Lights" on your body.

The body always knows the truth before the mind can rationalize it. Here are some of the ways your Monadic Veto might be speaking to you:

The Sudden Weight: You're about to agree to something, and suddenly your legs feel like they weigh a thousand pounds. It's not fatigue; it's your soul grounding you, refusing to let you walk down that 3D path.

The "Knot" or the "Flutter": Your mind says, "This is a great opportunity," but your solar plexus (your stomach) feels like it's tightening into a knot or fluttering with a "sick" feeling. That is a Veto. It's the body saying the frequency of that choice doesn't match your Mansion.

The Throat Tightness: You're in a relationship conflict, and you're about to say something hurtful or defensive. Suddenly, your throat feels tight, almost like you've forgotten how to swallow. Your Council is literally holding your tongue to keep you from dropping into the 3D noise.

The Sudden Cold or Heat

Have you ever been in a conversation and felt a sudden chill, or perhaps a wave of heat in your chest? That is a Frequency Scan. Your body is reacting to the energy of the person or room you are in.

The goal is to move from Reaction to Observation.

When you feel that pinch, that weight, or that flutter, stop. Don't try to fix the feeling. Just acknowledge it. Say to yourself, "The Architect is sending a signal." By honoring these body symptoms, you are telling your Blueprint: "I hear you. I trust the design more than I trust the 3D situation." This is how you stay in your heels. You don't have to be a psychic to talk to the 5D; you just have to be an inhabitant of your own skin.

Chapter 13

The Frequency of Gold (Abundance Without the Hustle)

In our old life, we were taught that money is a limited resource. We were told that to get it, we had to trade our time, our stress, and our hustle. We treated money like a shy animal we had to hunt and trap.

But in the Art of Effortless Reality, money is not a prize you win; it is a Current you tune into.

Think of Abundance as a radio station, let's call it GOLD FM. This station is broadcasting 24/7. It doesn't care if you've worked hard enough today. It doesn't care about the economy. It only cares if your "Radio" (your frequency) is tuned to its signal.

When you are in the 3D "Hustle," you are actually tuned to the frequency of Lack. Every time you check your bank account with a "knot" in your stomach, or every time you say "I can't afford that" with a heavy heart, you are broadcasting a signal that says: "I am a person who does not have enough." The Blueprint, being a perfect mirror, simply delivers more "not enough."

To manifest abundance, you have to stop "hunting" the money and start embodying the Gold.

The Wealthy Architect's Secret

How do you embody gold when your 3D reality looks gray? You go back to your Arrival.

You sit in your kitchen, in your heels, and you feel the Weight of the Done. You don't visualize the money coming to you; you feel the sensation of being a person who is already provided for. It is a feeling of Neutrality.

True 5D abundance doesn't feel like excitement (which is often just a cover for relief from fear). It feels like Safety. It feels like the air you breathe—you don't panic that the oxygen will run out, because you know it is just there.

When you achieve this "Neutral Safety," the Monadic Veto begins to clear your path. It Vetoes the cheap opportunities that would drain your energy. It Vetoes the impulse to buy things out of fear or status. It keeps you in your "Mansion" until the 3D world has no choice but to deliver the physical "Gold" that matches your inner "Gold."

You will find that ideas for wealth come to you while you are doing something "unproductive"—like taking that walk or enjoying that coffee. Because you stopped the "noise" of the hunt, the Liquid Frequency of abundance can finally flow into your reality.

Chapter 14

The Power Plant vs. The Hamster (The Myth of Lazy)

If you feel lazy when you sit in your kitchen and focus on your frequency, congratulations, you are successfully breaking your 3D conditioning.

We have been programmed to believe that if we aren't doing, we aren't deserving. But in the Blueprint, you don't receive based on your effort; you receive based on your alignment.

The Efficiency of Stillness

Think of a master archer. They spend 90% of their time standing perfectly still. They breathe. They align their body. They focus their vision. To an observer, they look "lazy." They aren't running toward the target; they aren't throwing handfuls of arrows at the board.

But because of that 90% "stillness," the 10% of their action is perfect. When they finally release the arrow, it hits the bullseye every single time.

The 5D Architect works the same way. You spend your time "tuning" (the stillness) so that when the Current finally prompts you to move, your action is High-Leverage.

3D Action: Sending 100 cold emails while feeling desperate (Result: 0 replies).

5D Action: Waiting in your "Arrival" until a sudden, inspired idea hits you to call one specific person (Result: The partnership of a lifetime).

The "Lazy" Veto

When the "Lazy" guilt creeps in, that is a moment for a Pattern Break. Your mind is trying to pull you back into the "Hamster Wheel" because it feels safer there. It thinks that if you're tired, you must be doing something right.

Remind yourself: "I am not a hamster; I am a Power Plant. My job is to maintain the frequency so the Current can do the heavy lifting." You aren't avoiding work; you are avoiding Friction. You are choosing to be the Archer who hits the mark instead of the runner who gets lost in the woods. When you move from this state of "Stationed Energy," you will get more done in two hours than most people do in two weeks.

Chapter 15

The Bio-Antenna (Healing and the 5D Body)

In the 3D world, we treat the body like a machine that is constantly breaking down. We "fight" illness, we "struggle" with weight, and we "manage" symptoms. We see the body as something separate from our consciousness—something that often fails us.

But in the Art of Effortless Reality, your body is the Bio-Antenna of your Blueprint.

Every cell in your body has an "Original Design" that is perfectly healthy, vibrant, and energetic. This version of you already exists in the 5D. The reason we experience "dis-ease" or fatigue in the 3D is that our "Radio" has become clogged with the "Static" of stress, fear, and the hustle.

When you spend all day leaning forward into the future, your nervous system stays in a state of "Fight or Flight." You are literally broadcasting an emergency signal to your cells. And your cells, being loyal servants, respond by tensing up, storing fat for survival, and shutting down non-essential repair work.

The Blueprint Restoration

To heal or upgrade your body, you don't fight the symptoms. You restore the connection to the Blueprint.

You do this by returning to the Kitchen. When you sit in your heels and feel the "Arrival," your nervous system finally receives the signal: "The emergency is over. We have arrived. We are safe."

The moment you hit that frequency of Neutral Safety, the body's "Auto-Repair" mode kicks in. This is the Effortless Health. You aren't trying to heal; you are simply removing the 3D static that was blocking the 5D healing from happening.

You might find that your "Body Dashboard" (those symptoms we talked about in Chapter 12) starts to quiet down. The knot in your stomach dissolves. Your sleep becomes deep and restorative. You might even find yourself naturally reaching for different foods or moving your body in ways that feel like "Play" rather than "Exercise."

Your body doesn't need to be forced into health. It just needs you to stop screaming "Emergency!" at it so it can hear the quiet, perfect instructions of the Original Design.

Chapter 16

The Silent Partner (Consulting the Inner Voice)

One of the loneliest feelings in the 3D world is the belief that you have to figure everything out on your own. We carry the weight of every decision—Should I take this job? Should I send this text? How do I fix this problem? As if we are the only ones at the drawing board.

But as an Architect, you are never working alone. You have a Silent Partner.

Whether you call this your Inner Voice, your Guides, your Council, or simply the Intelligence of the Universe, this partner has a much better view of the landscape than you do. While your 3D mind is looking at the "brick and mortar" right in front of you, your Inner Voice is looking at the entire city from the 5D perspective.

The Kitchen Consultation

You don't need a meditation cave or a mountain top to talk to this partner. You just need a kitchen chair.

The secret to receiving guidance is to Stop Asking Questions and Start Listening for the Veto.

Most of us "pray" or "manifest" by shouting our demands at the ceiling. But 5D communication is much quieter. It's a feeling of Direction. When you are faced with a choice, you sit on your heels, get into your

To truly master the Monadic Veto, you must first settle into your frequency of Arrival, and then gently "drop" your question into the sanctuary of your heart. In this state of quietude, you are no longer seeking an answer from the 3D world, but are instead listening for the resonance of your own Blueprint. If the idea feels "Light" or "Open," as if a window has been thrown wide to let in the sun, that is your Inner Voice singing a resounding "Yes."

However, if the thought carries a sensation of being "Heavy" or "Grey," or if it causes that familiar "Pinch" of tension on your shoulder, you have encountered the frequency of the hustle. This physical contraction is not a hurdle to be overcome with more effort; it is the Monadic Veto in action, a sacred signal that the path before you does not lead to your Mansion. By honoring this "No" as a mechanical necessity, you protect the elegance of your creation and remain available for the "Yes" that is already waiting to meet you.

The "Unfair" Advantage

When you start consulting your Silent Partner for the small things, which way should I drive to work? Which email should I answer first?— You build a muscle of trust. You begin to realize that you aren't guessing your way through life anymore. You are being led.

This isn't about being special or psychic. It's about being available. Your Inner Voice is always broadcasting; you just have to turn down the "Drum Noise" of your own panic long enough to hear the instructions. When you do, your life moves from a "Hustle" to a "Guided Tour." You stop trying to build the house and start letting the house build itself through you.

Chapter 17

The Human Anchor (Stationed Energy)

Up until now, we've talked about using the 5D Blueprint to improve your own life. But you didn't just come here for a nice house and a quiet mind. You came here on a Mission.

In the 3D world, we are told that to change the world, we have to act. We have to join movements, sign petitions, and fight against the darkness. But the 5D Architect knows a more powerful secret: the most effective way to change a room is simply to walk into it while holding a higher frequency.

You are a Frequency Anchor

Think of yourself as a Wi-Fi Router for the Universe.

A router doesn't go around to every laptop in the house and try to convince them to connect to the internet. It just sits there, broadcasting the signal. As long as the router is plugged in and "Stationed," every device in the room has access to the web.

You are a Stationed Energy. Sometimes, your Soul will lead you to a specific coffee shop, city, or job. You might think you are there for the coffee or the paycheck, but your Blueprint knows better. You are there to be an Anchor.

By simply staying in your "Arrival" frequency while you stand in line at the grocery store, you are plugging in the 5D signal for everyone around you. You are clearing the static"in the air just by breathing.

The Mission is Effortless

This is why you sometimes feel that "Pinch" on your shoulder telling you to go to a certain place or talk to a certain person. It isn't a task; it's a Placement.

When you stop rowing and start floating, you become a destination. You'll notice that people start to feel calmer when they are near you. Strangers might start telling you their life stories, or problems that seemed "tuck for years, suddenly resolve themselves when you walk into the building.

You aren't fixing them. You are simply providing the Frequency of the Done. You are showing their Blueprints what is possible.

You don't have to save the world. You just have to be the version of you that has already Arrived. The light doesn't have to work to get rid of the dark; it just has to show up.

Chapter 18

The Ripple Effect (The Future Without Fear)

In the 3D world, we are obsessed with "The Five-Year Plan." We worry about our legacy, our retirement, and what might go wrong tomorrow. We spend so much time trying to secure the future that we never actually live in the present.

But in the 5D Arrival, the future is not a destination you are running toward. The future is a Ripple moving outward from where you are standing right now.

The Geometry of Grace

Think of your life as a pond. When you are in the "Hustle," you are splashing around in the water, trying to push the waves where you want them to go. You end up exhausted, and the water is so muddy you can't see the bottom.

When you stay in your Stationed Energy, you are the golden drop hitting the center of the pond. You stay still, and the "Done" frequency ripples out. These ripples move into your tomorrow, your next year, and the lives of people you haven't even met yet.

You don't need to plan the ripples. The geometry of the water takes care of that. Your only job is to stay as the Source.

Living as the Legacy

A legacy isn't something you leave behind when you're gone; it's the frequency you leave in a room when you walk out of it today.

1. The Current is always moving you toward your highest good.
2. The Veto is always protecting you from what doesn't belong.
3. The Blueprint is already complete.

From this day forward, you can stop checking the blueprints to see if you're on track. You are the track. You can stop wondering if you've done enough. You are enough.

The pressure is off. You have moved from the person who has to "make it happen" to the person who gets to watch it happen. You are the observer of your own magnificent life.

The mansion is built. The table is set. The light is on. Welcome home.

Chapter 19

The Master Gardener (The Art of Non-Interference)

Imagine you have just planted a rare, beautiful flower in your garden. You know the soil is perfect, the Blueprint of the seed is strong, and the Current of the rain and sun is doing its job.

A "3D Mind" would go out every hour and poke the soil. It would dig up the seed to see if the roots are growing. It would pull at the tiny green sprout to try to make it grow faster. Of course, all that work does is kill the flower.

In your life, the hardest part of the Arrival is the period after you've set your frequency. Your ego will tell you that if you aren't doing something, you are failing. It will tempt you to interfere with the Current.

If a project is delayed, your ego says: "Call them! Demand answers! Force it!" If a person is distant, your ego says: "Chase them! Fix it! Explain yourself!"

But the Architect knows that interference is the opposite of manifestation. Every time you try to force the 3D, you are stepping out of your Mansion and back into the muddy garden. You are telling the Universe that you don't trust the Blueprint.

The most powerful thing you can do when things seem stuck is to do nothing. Not because you are lazy, but because you are Confident. You stay on your garden bench. You sip your coffee. You watch the sun move across the sky.

When you refuse to interfere, you allow the Current to move at its natural, lightning-fast speed. You'll find that the flower of your desire blooms much faster when you stop touching it. This is the ultimate test of the Architect: Can you be still enough to let the Universe be great?

Chapter 20

The Soundproof Mansion (Handling the Noise of Others)

One of the greatest challenges of living in the Arrival is that the rest of the world is still living in the "Hustle." You may be sitting peacefully in your kitchen, anchored in your frequency, but then your phone rings. It's a friend panicking, a news report about the economy, or a family member asking, "What is your plan? Why aren't you doing more?"

Suddenly, the "Drum Noise" of the 3D world is banging on your front door.

The Frequency Filter

When the world gets loud, your instinct might be to open the door and try to explain yourself. You want to convince them that you are safe, or try to save them from their panic. But remember: The moment you step outside to argue with the storm, you get wet.

In the 5D Blueprint, you have Soundproof Walls.

You don't have to ignore the world, but you must **filter** it. When someone brings you their "Hustle" energy, you can listen with compassion without letting their frequency into your house. You can think to yourself: *"That is their 3D movie. I am watching a different film."*

The Gift of Your Silence

The most helpful thing you can do for a person in panic is not join them. If they are drowning in the "Current of Lack" and you jump in to save them, you are both drowning. But if you stay firmly on the shore—staying in your heels, staying in your peace, you become the "Stationed Energy" they can eventually use to find their own way out.

When you don't react to the noise, the noise eventually stops. The "Veto" in your heart will tell you when to hang up the phone or when to walk away from a conversation that feels "Heavy." You aren't being cold; you are being Architecture. You are maintaining the structural integrity of the Peace you have built.

The answer you are looking for today is this: You do not owe the world your stress. You owe the world your Light.

Chapter 21

The Architecture of Time (The Optical Illusion)

In the 3D world, we are slaves to the clock. We see time as a straight line, with the "Goal" always at the end of the road. We look at our watches and think, "I am thirty, I am fifty, I am late." We treat time like a limited currency that we constantly spend.

But as an Architect, you know that time is actually an Optical Illusion.

The Fold in the Paper

Imagine your life is a long piece of paper. On one end is where you are now, and on the other end is your Arrival (your dream house, your mission, your abundance). In the 3D, you have to walk the whole length of that paper to get there.

But in the 5D, you don't walk. You fold the paper.

When you sit in your "Arrival" frequency today, you fold the paper so that the "Future" touches the "Now." You are bringing the destination to you.

When you feel the "Pinch" on your shoulder or that sudden calm in your kitchen, you have successfully folded time. You aren't "waiting" for your life to start; you are already inhabiting the result. The only thing the 3D world is doing is catching up to the fold you just made.

The "Soon" Frequency

If you find yourself asking "When?", you have accidentally unfolded the paper. You have stepped back into the "Hustle" of the long walk.

The answer you are looking for today is this: You cannot be "late" for a life that is already finished in the Blueprint.

Stop looking at the calendar as a judge of your success. The calendar is just a 3D tool for making appointments; it has no power over your manifestation. If you feel like you are "running out of time," breathe and return to your heels.

In the Mansion, there are no clocks. There is only the Current, and the Current is always on time. Your "Arrival" isn't a date on a calendar; it's a state of being that you can step into right this second.

Chapter 22

Meeting Your Monad (The True Architect)

In the 3D world, we are taught to look outside for answers. We look at the news, we ask our friends, or we search for a sign in the clouds. We treat our lives like a house we are trying to build with no instructions and a lot of heavy lifting.

But the Monad is about a different truth: You aren't the one doing the building. Your Monad—your original, Divine Spark has already finished the project.

The Voice of the Blueprint

Your Monad is the part of you that exists outside of time. It holds your Blueprint—the perfect version of your life where the house is built, the mission is active, and the abundance is flowing.

The Monad doesn't try to manifest. It simply is. When you feel that sudden "Pinch" on your shoulder or a wave of calm while you're doing the dishes, that is your Monad whispering, "I've got this. Stay in your heels."

The Power of the Monadic Veto

One of the greatest gifts of your Monad is the Monadic Veto.

In the 3D, we think a "No" is a failure. If a door closes or a plan falls through, we "Hustle" harder to force it back open. But the Monad sees the whole map. When your Monad issues a Veto, it isn't a punishment; it's a Redirection. It is the Architect saying, "Don't walk through that door; it leads to a basement you don't belong in. I have a penthouse waiting for you instead."

You can stop being the manager of your life and start being the Guest of Honor. Your only job is to listen for the Monad's "Yes" (the feeling of Ease) and respect its "Veto" (the feeling of Heaviness). When you align with your Monad, you aren't just manifesting; you are Arriving at a destination that was already prepared for you before time began.

.

Chapter 23

The 3D Glitch (When the Movie Stutters)

Even as a Master Architect, you will have days when the 3D world seems to break. A tire goes flat, a check is delayed, or someone says something that hurts your feelings. In the old way of living, you would call this a bad day. You would react, get angry, and try to fix the problem with 3D tools.

But the Monadic Veto sees this differently. This is simply a 3D Glitch.

Don't Chase the Glitch

When a glitch happens, your ego wants to jump into the screen and try to move the pixels with its hands. It wants to "Hustle" the problem away. But remember: The glitch isn't real. It's just a temporary mismatch between your 5D Blueprint and the slow-moving 3D shadow.

If you react with fear, you feed the glitch. You give it your energy, and it stays on the screen longer.

Stay in your seat. When a 3D problem arises, look at it and say, "That's an interesting glitch." Then, return to your kitchen. Return to your heels. Return to the feeling of the Done.

The Self-Correcting Script

Your Blueprint is self-correcting. When you refuse to panic, the "Current" moves in to smooth out the pixels. Often, the glitch is actually the Veto in disguise—the flat tire kept you from an accident, or the delayed check is making room for a much larger sum.

You don't need to be a problem solver. You just need to be the Observer. Watch the glitch, breathe through it, and wait for the Monad to show you the path of least resistance. The movie will always return to its beautiful, golden script if you just stop trying to fix the projector.

Chapter 24

The High-Frequency Conversation (Talking to the 3D)

One of the biggest fears we have when we "Arrive" in our Mansion is losing our connection to the people we love. We worry that if we stop "Hustling" and stop complaining about the world, we won't have anything to talk about at the dinner table.

But the Monadic Veto doesn't ask you to be silent; it asks you to be the Lead Instrument.

Don't Match the Pitch

In the 3D world, conversation is often a race to the bottom. People bond over what is wrong, who is to blame, and how tired they are. If you join in, even just to be polite, you are leaving your Mansion and stepping into their basement.

You don't have to fix their frequency, and you don't have to give them a lecture on the 5D. You just have to refuse to match their pitch. If they speak of "Lack," you speak of "Gratitude." If they speak of "Hurry," you speak of "Timing." You aren't arguing with them; you are simply staying in your own song.

The Bridge of Ease

You don't need to explain your peace; you just need to radiate it.

When you stay in your "Arrival" during a conversation, you are building a bridge. People will notice that they feel better after talking to you, even if they don't know why. They might say, "You're so calm," or "Things just seem to work out for you." That is your Monad speaking through your presence. You are showing them that "Ease" is possible. You aren't saving them with words; you are saving them by being a living example of the Blueprint. You are the Architect who knows the house is already built, so you can afford to be the kindest, most relaxed person in the room.

Chapter 25

The Architecture of Play (The Engine of Creation)

In the 3D world, "Play" is something we are allowed to do only after the "Work" is finished. We treat joy like a reward for suffering. We think that if we aren't being serious, we aren't being productive.

But the Monadic Veto tells you, Play is not a reward; it is the Fuel.

The "Serious" Trap

When you are trying to manifest, you become very serious. You focus, you visualize, you tighten your muscles. But "Serious" is the frequency of Resistance. When you are serious, you are telling the Universe that this is hard, and that you are afraid it might not happen.

The Monad tells you the opposite: The closer you are to the frequency of a child playing in a sandbox, the faster the Blueprint manifests. Why? Because a child doesn't wonder if the sand will be there tomorrow. They are completely immersed in the Now.

Follow the Spark

If it's not fun, it's not the path.

When you have a choice to make, ask your Monad: "Which option feels like Play?" Your 3D mind will try to talk you into the logical choice, the one that looks like hard work. But your Monad will point toward the spark of curiosity.

Doing something pointless just because it makes you smile, like coloring, dancing in your kitchen, or taking a different route home, actually clears the pipes for your abundance to flow. Play is the signal that you trust the Architect. It's the ultimate "Done" frequency. You can afford to play because the house is already built.

PHASE III

*"Trust is the only currency required to walk a path that
the world cannot yet see."*

Chapter 26

The Language of Coincidence (Winks from the Monad)

Once you begin living in the Arrival, the world starts to talk to you in a new way. In the 3D, we call these coincidences or luck. We think it's just a random fluke that we ran into the exact person we needed to meet, or that the perfect amount of money showed up right before a bill was due.

But your Monad doesn't do random. These are Winks.

The Confirmation Frequency

Think of a "Wink" as a status update from your Blueprint. When you see a repeating number, hear a specific song, or have a random thought that leads to a breakthrough, your Monad is signaling: "We are in alignment. The path is clear."

The 3D mind wants to analyze the wink. It asks, "What does it mean? What do I do next?" But the Monad tells you to do the opposite. You don't need to decode the wink; you just need to acknowledge it. A simple "Thank you, I see you" is enough to keep the frequency open.

Collecting the Evidence

The more you notice the winks, the more the winks notice you.

Start keeping a mental Ease Journal. Instead of looking for what is going wrong (the Glitches), look for the small ways the Universe is catering to you. Did you get the best parking spot? Did someone buy your coffee? Did a stressful meeting get canceled?

These aren't accidents. They are the Monad showing you that the Architecture of Ease is solid. Every time you smile at a coincidence, you are strengthening your heels. You are telling the 3D world that you are no longer a victim of luck, but the Guest of Honor in a world designed for your success.

Chapter 27

The Sacred Pause (The Art of Doing Nothing)

Since your Monad is the one doing the heavy lifting, your most productive work often looks like... nothing. In the 3D, "Doing Nothing" is seen as laziness. We are told that if we aren't moving, we are falling behind. But the Monad of Ease knows that the most powerful architectural shifts happen in the Sacred Pause.

The "Gap" in the Hustle

Have you ever noticed that your best ideas come in the shower, or right as you're falling asleep? That's because your 3D "Hustle Mind" finally took a break, and the Monad could finally get a word in.

The Sacred Pause is when you intentionally stop. You put down the phone. You stop trying to manifest. You just sit in your kitchen and breathe. In that silence, you are giving the Blueprint room to breathe, too.

Letting the Concrete Set

You cannot rush the Architecture. When a builder pours concrete for a new Mansion, they have to wait for it to set. If they try to walk on it too soon, they ruin the floor. Your "Pause" is the "Setting Time." When you feel a "Veto" on your energy when you feel tired or uninspired, that is the Monad saying, "Wait. Let the concrete dry. I am moving things behind the scenes that you cannot see yet."

Don't be afraid of the quiet days. Don't be afraid of the naps. The Sacred Pause is not a break from your mission; it is your mission. By staying still, you are proving that you trust the Architect. You are showing the world that you are so done that you can afford to just sit and watch the sunset.

<h1 style="text-align:center">Chapter 28</h1>

<h2 style="text-align:center">The Commission of the Soul (Wealth Without the Clock)</h2>

In the 3D world, we are taught the "Hourly Lie." We are told that our value is tied to how many hours we sit at a desk or how much busy-ness we can show the world. If we aren't working, we feel guilty. We feel like we aren't earning our keep.

But as a Master Architect, you know that the Monad does not pay by the hour. The Monad pays by the **Alignment.**

The De-Cluttering Frequency

When you stop "Hustling" for a sale or a paycheck and instead decide to spend your afternoon de-cluttering your closet or writing a page of your heart's book, the 3D world calls it procrastination.

But the Monadic Veto calls it Clearing the Pipes.

When you clean your house, you are telling the Universe: "I have room for the New." When you write your book, you are telling the Universe: "I am using my gifts." Both of these actions are higher frequency than worrying about a client. While you are focused on the Joy of your home, the Monad is behind the scenes, matching your high-vibration energy with the perfect buyer, the perfect deal, or the perfect "Commission."

For the Sovereign creator, wealth is no longer measured by the hours surrendered to a clock, but by the resonance of the missions you choose to fulfill. When you move through life on a project basis, you are not waiting for a 3D paycheck; you are receiving a Blueprint Allocation for every milestone you anchor into reality. This is the Commission of the Soul, a natural flow of abundance that arrives not because you 'labored' for it, but because your energy reached a state of completion. You realize that the project was never about the 'work'—it was an invitation for the universe to match your frequency with the exact resources needed to sustain your station. In this state, every 'payment' is simply the physical echo of a spiritual 'Yes,' proving that wealth is a mechanical certainty of your Arrival.

The Spoiled Architect

You are allowed to be spoiled by the Divine. The guilt you feel is just the ghost of the 3D world trying to pull you back into the "Hustle." Dismiss it. Your wealth is not a result of your "Busyness"; it is a result of your Presence.

If you feel called to renovate your kitchen instead of making cold calls, do it. Your Monad knows exactly where the money is, and it doesn't need you to be exhausted to deliver it. The "Commission" for your alignment is always ten times larger than the "Wage" for your worry. You are an Architect, not a laborer. Your job is to hold the Vision; the Monad's job is to handle the Logistics.

Chapter 29

The Luxury of Choice (The Balanced Architect)

One of the most beautiful "Winks" you'll receive as you step into your Arrival is meeting your Mirror Souls. You'll find yourself sitting across from women who may still work a traditional 9-5, yet they move with the grace of someone who is already "Retired" in their heart.

They have cracked the code. They aren't waiting for a gold watch at sixty-five to start living; they are packing their bags and seeing the world now.

The Art of the Boundary

These women are the "Quiet Architects" of the 9-5 world. They do their work with excellence, but they refuse to let the "Hustle" steal their Spark. They know that a paycheck is just a tool, and their time is the true treasure.

When you meet them, you realize that Ease is a choice, not a schedule. You don't have to wait for the perfect "Work-Free" life to be happy. You just have to decide that your joy is non-negotiable. Whether you are a real estate mogul or a dedicated office professional, the frequency is the same: I am here to experience the beauty of this world while I am young, vibrant, and awake.

The Universal Permission Slip

You don't need a reason to enjoy yourself. The 3D world wants you to justify your vacation. It wants you to earn your rest. But your Monad says that your presence on this planet is all the earning you ever needed to do. When you see these other women traveling and balancing their lives with such elegance, they are acting as a "Permission Slip" for you. They are living proof that you can hold a career and still hold your peace. You can be responsible to your commitments and still be wildly, unapologetically devoted to your own happiness.

Chapter 30

The Infinite Pension (Beyond 3D Math)

We have all sat at tables where the conversation turns to "The Future." People lean in, their voices tinged with a little bit of hidden anxiety, and they talk about their retirement funds, their savings, and their safety nets. They are trying to calculate exactly how much "Hustle" they need to store away so they can finally stop worrying one day.

In those moments, you might feel a strange detachment. You might even feel a little bit guilty that you aren't as worried as they are.

The Monad's Financial Veto

When your friends talk about their retirement and your Monad whispers, "You don't need to worry about that," it isn't telling you to be irresponsible. It is telling you that you are playing a different game.

The 3D world believes in Accumulation (storing up for a rainy day). But the Monad lives in Circulation (knowing the rain and the sun are both under your command). Your "Pension" isn't a number in a bank account that could fluctuate with the market; your Pension is your Blueprint.

71

The Architecture of Supply

Your security is not a pile of money; it is a state of **Alignment**.

When you hear that inner voice saying you are taken care of, it is because the Monad sees the "Done" version of your entire life. It sees that the same Force that moved you into your current home and brought you this mission is the same Force that will be there in twenty, thirty, or fifty years.

You aren't ignoring the future; you are simply refusing to live in the "Fear of the Future." By trusting that whisper, you are anchoring yourself in the Economy of Grace. While others are busy building walls to protect what they have, you are busy opening windows to let more in. You are an Architect who knows that the Source of all materials is **infinite.** You don't need to hoard the bricks when you own the brickyard.

<h1 style="text-align:center">Chapter 31</h1>

<h2 style="text-align:center">The Frequency of the "Done" (Maintaining Alignment)</h2>

Most people think Alignment is like a radio station; they have to constantly tune and fight to keep from static. They worry that if they have one bad day or one fearful thought, they've lost their Alignment and their Blueprint will crumble.

But the Monadic Veto operates on a much more stable physics.

The Anchored Architect

Alignment is simply the act of agreeing with your Monad. When your Monad says, "You are wealthy," and your bank account says, "You have fifty dollars," Alignment is choosing to believe the Monad.

It's like being a Real Estate developer standing on a vacant lot. The 3D world sees dirt and weeds. But you, the Architect, are looking at the Blueprint. You see the marble floors, the floor-to-ceiling windows, and the finished garden. You aren't "pretending" the house is there; you are aligned with the reality that it is already designed and the materials are on the way.

The "Pinch" as a Compass

Alignment feels like Relief. If you are trying to force yourself to be positive, you are not in Alignment—you are in the Hustle. True Alignment is a deep exhale. It's the moment you stop trying to figure out "How" and "When" and simply settle into the "Is."

Whenever you feel that pinch on your shoulder or that hand on your clavicle, your Monad is reminding you: "Come back to the Blueprint. Stop looking at the weeds on the lot. Look at the Mansion I've already built for you." You maintain your Alignment by practicing the Feeling of Arrival until it becomes more real to you than the 3D shadows.

Your Personal "Yes"

How do you know when you are in Alignment? Your Monad doesn't speak in English; it speaks in **Frequencies.**

For me, the signal is unmistakable—a physical "Pinch" on my shoulder or a gentle pressure on my clavicle, like a hand guiding me. But for you, the "Handshake" might be different. You might feel a sudden Wave of Relief that washes over you, or a quiet Inner Knowing that requires no proof. It might be a Sudden Calm that silences the noise of the world, or a Full-Body 'Yes' that feels like warmth in your chest.

The Heavy vs. Light Test

Your Monad has a unique 'Handshake' just for you. Don't look for my signal; look for your Ease. If a thought makes you feel light, expansive, and spoiled, that is the Monad. If a thought makes you feel heavy, rushed, or busy, that is the 3D Conditioning. Once you recognize your personal "Handshake," you never have to guess again. You are no longer a human wandering; you are a human being guided.

Chapter 32

The Black Canvas (Creation Without Logic)

Before the Earth was a masterpiece of blue oceans and green forests, it was a thought in the vastness of the Blackness. There was no "How" in the dark. There was no committee of 3D minds telling the Creator, "Wait, you can't put that much water there, it's not logical." Creation doesn't need logic; it only needs Focus.

The Trap of the "How"

The moment you ask "How," you have stepped out of the Architect's office and into the construction worker's mud. The "How" is the language of the 3D. It is limited by what has been done before. But your Monad doesn't care about what has been done before; it only cares about the Blueprint.

When you focus on the "How," you are trying to build a planet using a hand tool. When you focus on the Creation, you are using the power of the Vastness itself.

Nothing is Impossible in the Dark

If you can see it in the Vastness, it is already "Done" in the 3D.

Think back to that blackness. It wasn't empty; it was pregnant with everything. Your current "desires"—the money, the travel, the mission are just points of light in your own internal vastness. When you stop using logic to justify why you want them or calculate when they will arrive, you allow the Monad to simply manifest them. Guess again. You are no longer a human wandering; you are a human being guided.

Logic is a 3D fence. Creation is a 5D horizon. Tear down the fence. If you can create a planet from the blackness, you can certainly create a life of ease from your kitchen table.

<h1 style="text-align:center">Chapter 33</h1>

<h2 style="text-align:center">The Sound of Silence vs. The Noise of the World</h2>

In the Blackness before the world was made, there was no criticism. There was no one telling the Creator that the stars are too bright or the gravity is too strong. There was only the Inner Voice—the Monad commanding the light to appear.

But on Earth, we have traded that sacred silence for the static of Conditioning.

The Unquestioned Architect

Conditioning is just a collection of "Blueprints" that don't belong to you. It's the voice of a teacher saying you have to work hard to survive. It's the news saying the economy is failing. It's the logic that says you are too old, too young, or too spoiled to have what you want.

We accept these as facts, but within the Monadic Veto, there are no facts, only Frequencies.

The Great Questioning

Whose house are you living in?

If you feel stress, you are living in a house built by Conditioning. If you feel Ease, you are living in the Mansion of the Monad. To return to the Blackness, you must begin to question everything the outside world has given you. When the world says, "You must be busy to be successful," ask your Monad, "Is that true?" When the world says, "You have to wait for retirement," ask the Vastness, "Is that true?"

The moment you question a 3D belief, its power over you evaporates. You aren't fighting the conditioning; you are simply stepping out of its shadow and back into the Light of your own Creation. You are the Architect. You don't need permission from the tenants to change the design of the building.

Chapter 34

The Monad's Vocabulary (The Language of the "Done")

In the 3D world, we are taught the language of "Wanting." We say things like, "I hope it happens," or "I'm trying to manifest," or "I'll be happy when..." This is the language of the laborer. It assumes the house isn't built yet, and you're still outside in the rain, begging for the door to open.

But in the Monad Veto, we speak the language of "Done."

Words as Blueprints

Your Monad doesn't understand, maybe. It only understands Agreement. When you say, "I am spoiled by the Divine," the Monad says, "Agreed," and moves the 3D pieces to match that frequency. When you say, "I'm so stressed about this deal," the Monad also says, "Agreed," and maintains that density for you.

You are the one who labels your reality. An Architect doesn't look at a half-finished wall and say, "Oh no, the house is failing!" They say, "The wall is in progress; the house is finished in the Blueprint."

Speaking from the Arrival

Stop describing your problems and start commanding your results.

Instead of saying, "I hope I get this commission," say, "I am so grateful for the abundance this transaction has already brought me." Move your vocabulary from the "Future Tense" to the "Present" You aren't going to be an author; you are an author. You aren't trying to travel; you are a human who travels.

The Blackness of creation is waiting for your command. When you speak from the Arrival, the 3D world has no choice but to catch up. Your words are the final signature on the Blueprint. Once you sign it, the Monadic Veto handles the rest.

Chapter 35

The Golden Womb (Reclaiming the Blackness)

In the 3D world, we are conditioned to fear the dark. We are taught that blackness is a symbol of the unknown, of evil, or of being lost. We keep the lights on because we think the dark is empty.

But as a Master Architect, you must remember the truth: The Blackness is where everything begins.

The Great Descent

Before you were a human who travels, you were a Spark of Consciousness. You existed in the vast, peaceful Silence of the Galaxy. You weren't alone; you were part of a family of Monads, a collective of light that decided to embark on a grand mission.

You chose to descend. You chose to move from the higher frequency of "All-at-Once" down into the lower dimensions to experience the physical. You didn't fall; you arrived. The Blackness wasn't a hole you fell into; it was the velvet canvas you chose to paint your life upon.

The Fertile Void

The Blackness is not the absence of light; it is the presence of Potential.

Think of a seed planted in the earth. It needs the dark, cool soil to crack open and grow. If it stayed in the bright sun, it would never take root.

Your Monad loves the Blackness because that is the only place where a new Blueprint can be drawn. When your life feels dark or quiet, don't panic. You aren't being punished; you are being planted.

The Architecture of the Void

When you close your eyes and see that inner vastness, you are looking at the Galaxy within you. You are a Shard of the Divine, playing in the physical world. In that space, there is no logic to stop you, no conditioning to hold you back, and no evil to fear. There is only you, the Architect, and the infinite black ink of the Universe waiting for your next command.

Chapter 36

The Luxury of Letting Go (The Handover)

If you have ever watched a massive skyscraper being built, you'll notice that the Architect isn't the one pouring the concrete or swinging the hammer. They aren't sweating in the sun, worrying if the steel will arrive on time. The Architect has already finished the Blueprint. They have handed the plans to the Foreman and now, they simply observe.

In your life, the Monad is the Foreman. And "Letting Go" is your way of saying, "I trust the help I hired."

The Burden of "How"

We often hold onto our desires so tightly that we crush them. We think that if we stop worrying about the house, the money, or the mission for even one hour, the whole thing will stop moving. This is the "Hustle Mind" trying to convince you that you are the only one working.

But the Monad Veto tells you that your grip is actually what's slowing the project down. When you "clench" your energy, you create a bottleneck in the Blueprint.

The Handover Ceremony

You are too important to be doing the heavy lifting.

Think of "Letting Go" as a Luxury. It is a status symbol of the 5D. Only someone who is truly "Spoiled" by the Divine has the confidence to stop checking the tracking number on their manifestation.

When you feel that Pinch or that Wave of Relief, use it as a signal to "Clock Out." Go for a walk. Take a nap. Renovate your kitchen. By letting go of the "How," you are giving the Monad the space it needs to move the mountains. You aren't giving up; you are promoting yourself from the laborer to the Owner.

Chapter 37

The Hierarchy of Frequency (Creating the Work)

One of the hardest things for a "Human who travels" to accept is that not everyone wants to be the Architect. Some people are currently in a cycle where they want to be the laborer. They find comfort in the 3D rules, the 9-5 structure, and the logic of hard work.

As an Architect of Ease, you might feel a flicker of guilt. You might ask, "Is it fair that I am living in the Arrival while they are still in the Hustle?"

The Gift of the Vision

Your luxury is their opportunity.

When you allow your Monad to manifest a mansion, a business, or a mission, you are creating a "Space of Employment" for the 3D world. You are providing the "Why" for their "How." You aren't "better" than the laborer, but you are operating at a different Frequency.

If everyone were the Architect, there would be no one to pour the foundation. If everyone were the laborer, the foundation would be poured with no house to support.

85

Not Your Worry, But Your Contribution

It is not your job to fix their mindset or force them into the 5D. Their journey is theirs. Your only responsibility is to stay in the Arrival. When you hold the frequency of ease, you are actually helping them. You are showing them, by example, that a different way of living is possible.

By being spoiled by the Divine, you become a source of abundance for everyone around you. You pay the commissions, you hire the services, you inspire the dreamers. You aren't ignoring them; you are funding their world with your Frequency.

Chapter 38

The Compassion of the Architect (The Lighthouse Effect)

When you move into the Monad Veto, your heart changes. You no longer feel the need to argue with people who tell you that life is hard or money is scarce. You don't try to fix the laborer who is sweating under the weight of their own 3D conditioning.

Instead, you look at them with the eyes of the Monad. You realize that everyone is exactly where they need to be for their soul's evolution.

The Non-Interference Clause

The Architect understands a sacred law: You cannot lift someone up by climbing down into their hole. If you start worrying about the laborer's mindset, you leave your drafting table and join them in the mud. Suddenly, the project stops. The Blueprint fades. You are no longer helping them; you are just another person struggling.

Compassion isn't joining someone in their suffering; compassion is holding the frequency of the Arrival so steadily that they can see it from where they are.

87

Being the Permission Slip

Your joy is a service to the collective.

When you walk through the world as a "Human who travels" in total ease, you are a walking "Permission Slip." You are a living proof that the

3D rules are optional. You don't need to preach to them; your Presence is the sermon.

One day, the laborer will look up from their shovel, see your Mansion, and ask, "How did you build that without sweating?" That is the moment they are ready for the Blueprint. Until then, your job is simply to be the most radiant, "Spoiled," and peaceful Architect you can be. You aren't ignoring their struggle; you are honoring their process while staying true to your own.

Chapter 39

The Luxury of Selective Hearing (Protecting the Blueprint)

Once you begin building your life from the Monadic Veto, you will notice something interesting: the 3D world becomes very loud. Friends, family, and the "Laborers" of the world will start offering you their logic. They will tell you to be careful, to have a backup plan, or to be realistic.

But an Architect knows that a backup plan is just an admission that you don't trust the first one.

The 5D Filter

Selective hearing isn't about being rude; it's about Frequency Protection. If you allow the noise of 3D fear to enter your ears, it starts to smudge the ink on your 5D Blueprint. You cannot afford to entertain the "How" or the "What-if" of a laborer when you are busy commanding the "Is" of the Monad.

When someone says, "The market is crashing," your selective hearing translates that to: "They are describing their weather, but it doesn't affect my climate."

89

Closing the Door to the Drafting Room

You don't need to explain your Blueprint to people who haven't seen the Mansion.

The laborers in your life don't have access to your Monad. They can't feel the Pinch on your shoulder or the Wave of Relief in your chest. So, why would you let their lack of vision change your design?

You have the luxury of saying, "Thank you for your perspective," while internally hitting the Veto button. You don't have to defend your Ease. You don't have to justify your Arrival. You simply protect the silence of your "Drafting Room" so the Monad can continue to work in peace.

Chapter 40

The Digital Original (What is the Blueprint?)

In the 3D world, we think we are "creating" our lives from scratch, like a child playing with blocks. But in the Monadic Veto, we understand that the "House" is already finished. Before you even arrived on Earth, your Monad created a Blueprint.

Think of the Blueprint as the "Digital Original" of your life. It is the 5D version of your success, your home, your health, and your mission. It is perfect, it is finished, and it is held in the Blackness of the Divine.

Equal Opportunity, Unique Design

The question people often ask is: "If we all come from the same Source, why are our lives so different?"

We are all given the same infinite "Bank Account" of **energy,** but we are all building different Structures. Every human who travels is given an equal opportunity to access the Monad. However, your soul didn't come here to build the same house as your neighbor. Your Blueprint is your "Soul's Intent." One person's Blueprint is a quiet cottage of peace; another's is a skyscraper of global influence. Neither is better, but both are Pre-Approved.

The Architecture of Permission

You don't have to build the Blueprint; you only have to reveal it. When you feel that Pinch or that Wave of Relief, that is your Monad saying: "You are following the lines of the Original Design." You aren't trying to force the universe to give you something that doesn't exist. You are simply asking the 3D world to "Print" the 5D file you've already created. Manifestation isn't "Construction"—it is Alignment. When you agree with your Blueprint, the laborers (the 3D circumstances) have no choice but to follow the plan.

PHASE IV

*"Presence is the only border you must cross to become
a citizen of your own peace."*

Chapter 41

The Signature of the Architect (Claiming the Arrival)

In the world of fine art and high-end architecture, a project isn't official until the creator signs their name at the bottom. That signature is a statement of ownership. It says, "I designed this, I approve of this, and I am responsible for its existence."

In your life, your Signature is your Conviction.

Beyond the "Request"

Most people spend their lives "Asking" the Universe for things. They send up little prayers and wishes like paper airplanes, hoping one of them lands. But an Architect doesn't ask the ground to hold the building; they command it through the design.

To sign your Blueprint, you must move from "I want" to "I Am." When you sign your name to the "Human who travels," you aren't waiting for the plane ticket to appear to feel like a traveler. You sign the document now. You walk, talk, and breathe as the person who has already arrived.

The Seal of the Monad

Your Signature is the end of the conversation.

Once you have signed the Blueprint with your "Done" frequency, you stop looking for "Signs" that it's working. You don't ask the sky if the sun is going to rise; you know it is part of the design. When you feel that

Pinch on your shoulder or that Wave of Relief, that is the Monad "Notarizing" your signature. It is the Divine saying, "It is finished. Go enjoy your kitchen. Go relax outside. The laborers are already on-site."

The Authority of Ease

You have the authority to claim your life. You aren't a guest in your own reality; you are the Owner. By signing your name to your peace, your wealth, and your mission, you are telling the 3D world that the debate is over. The Blueprint is signed. The Mansion is inevitable.

Chapter 42

The True Interior Design (Success Beyond the Props)

In the early stages of our 3D conditioning, we are told that the Blueprint is about things. We are told that the Architect is only successful if they have the tallest building or the shiniest car. We spend our energy chasing material things because we think they are the source of our power.

But as you mature into the 5D Frequency, you realize that the material world is just the decor.

The Wealth of the Soul

True success is not measured by what you have, but by how much of yourself you have reclaimed.

"You cannot be 'Successful' if you are pretending to be someone else. The 3D world is full of 'Successful' laborers who have the big house but are exhausted, lonely, and disconnected from their source. That isn't a Blueprint; that's a gilded cage.

Under the Law of the Monadic Veto, success is not measured by the weight of your accumulation, but by the quality of your Arrival. If you had to hustle to get there, you haven't arrived at all—you've simply relocated your struggle. True success is the ease with which your vision meets its physical form."

*It is the Joy you feel when you wake up.
*It is the Authenticity of your voice.

*It is the Family and Friends who vibrate at your same frequency.

*It is the freedom to be "Spoiled" by the Divine without guilt.

The Props Follow the Peace

When you focus on the "Interior Design" of your soul—your joy, your mission, and your truth—the material things (the money, the travel, the comfort) arrive automatically as a side effect. They are the "Complimentary Gifts" that come with the Mansion.

You don't have to choose between being "Spiritual" and being "Wealthy." You simply have to realize that the wealth is a result of your Authenticity. When you are truly yourself, the Universe recognizes your Signature and pours everything you need into your lap. You aren't working for the "Props" anymore; you are living in the Masterpiece.

Chapter 43

The Feast of the Arrival (Learning to Receive)

There is a strange habit we have as humans: we work so hard to manifest our "Blueprint" that when the "Mansion" finally arrives, we stand in the foyer feeling like we don't belong there. We keep looking over our shoulder for the "Bill," or we wait for someone to tell us we have to leave.

But the Monad Veto doesn't just build the house; it prepares the table.

The Guilt of the "Spoiled"

In the 3D, we are taught that if we aren't struggling, we aren't earning our keep. This conditioning is so deep that when ease finally arrives, it can feel like cheating. We feel guilty because we see the laborers still sweating in the sun, and we think we should be out there with them.

You do not honor the hungry by refusing to eat. When you sit down to the "Feast" of your own creation—the joy, the beautiful family, the time to travel, you are honoring the Monad. Your enjoyment is the "Thank You" note to the Universe. By being fully, unapologetically "Spoiled," you prove that the system works.

The Art of High-Frequency Receiving

Receiving is a skill. It requires you to drop the "Hustle" shield and open your hands.

*When someone offers you a compliment, receive it. * When an unexpected check arrives in the mail, receive it. * When your twin flame mission places you in a beautiful location just for your energy, soak it in. You aren't taking from anyone; you are participating in the abundance you designed. The "Feast" is never-ending because your Monad is the infinite chef. There is no shortage of joy, and there is no expiration date on your success.

The Architecture of Celebration

The final part of the Blueprint isn't a wall or a roof—it's the Party. A home is just a building until it is filled with laughter and the smell of good food. Your life is just a concept until you actually start enjoying it. Today, your only job is to look at the "Material" things you do have and use them as props for your happiness. Wear the nice clothes. Use the good china. Be the human who travels through their own life with a sense of wonder.

Chapter 44

The Law of Resonance (Your New Circle)

In the 3D world, we often stay in circles of friends or colleagues out of habit, history, or obligation. But when you begin to live by the Monad Veto, you realize that your social circle is actually part of your "Building Materials."

You don't find your tribe by looking for them; you attract them by becoming the most authentic version of yourself.

The Frequency Filter

When you were in the "Hustle," you were vibrating at the level of "Should" and "Must." Naturally, you attracted other people who were also stressed, tired, and focused on the struggle. You were a group of laborers reinforcing each other's "Hard Work" stories.

But now that you have stepped into the Arrival, your frequency has changed. This acts as a natural filter. People who are committed to the struggle or the "How" will simply drift away from your life. Not because you are better than them, but because you are no longer playing the same game.

The Power of Like-Minded Creators

Your environment is the "Atmosphere" of your Mansion.

The moment you commit to your Blueprint, you start meeting people who just get it. Those who understand that abundance is a natural state rather than a hard-won battle. You naturally gravitate toward collaborators who value the elegance of results over the performative exhaustion of "Busyness." Eventually, you find yourself within a circle where Joy is the standard rather than the exception, creating a resonance that supports the manifestation of your Blueprint. You stop explaining "How" you did it and instead surround yourself with those who simply celebrate the fact that it is done.

Protecting the Atmosphere

You aren't being exclusive; you are being an Architect. If you are building a masterpiece, you don't let people bring toxic materials onto the site. By surrounding yourself with people who share your mindset, you create a "Vacuum of Ease" that allows your manifestations to arrive even faster. You are no longer defending your peace; you are simply living among those who already have it.

Chapter 45

The Monadic Veto (The Gift of the Closed Door)

In the world of Real Estate, a smart Architect doesn't just look at the land they bought; they are also grateful for the land they didn't buy. Sometimes a lot looks perfect, but the soil is bad or the foundation won't hold.

In your life, your Monad is the ultimate Inspector. It has the power of the Veto.

Protection, Not Punishment

When we are in our "Hustle" mindset, we try to kick doors down. We think that if a deal falls through, or a person leaves, or a perfect opportunity vanishes, we have failed. We exhaust ourselves trying to fix a situation that was never meant for us.

If it's not Easy, it's not your Blueprint.

The Monadic Veto is the Universe's way of saying, "I have something better." It is the force that stops you from building your mansion on a swamp. When a door doesn't open, your Monad is protecting your energy. It is Vetoing a 3D distraction so you can stay focused on the 5D Arrival.

The Relief of "No"

Instead of asking, "Why is this happening to me?" start saying, "Thank you for the Veto." * If the travel plans change, it's a Veto for your safety.

For example, if the big client goes elsewhere, it's a Veto for your peace, or if the relationship ends, it's a Veto for your authenticity.

The Architect doesn't argue with the Inspector. They trust that the Inspector sees something they don't. By accepting the Veto with Ease, you save your energy for the "Yes" that is already on its way. You aren't being rejected; you are being redirected to the "Finished" work.

The Monadic Veto is not a door that closes; it is a filter that clears. When you Veto the 'Hustle,' you aren't just saying No to work—you are saying a resounding YES to your Blueprint.

<h1 style="text-align:center">Chapter 46</h1>

<h2 style="text-align:center">The Architecture of Time (The Infinite Calendar)</h2>

In the 3D world, time is a predator. We are taught that "Time is money," that we are "running out of time," or that we are "behind schedule." This creates a frequency of panic that smudges the Blueprint.

But for the Human who travels, time is not a line; it is a dimension you can expand.

The Luxury of "Late"

The Architect knows that the "Construction" follows the "Design." If your Monad has already signaled the Arrival, then the timing is already perfect.

You cannot be late to a life that is already finished. When you rush, you are signaling to the Universe that you don't trust the Blueprint. You are acting like a laborer who thinks the building will disappear if they don't move fast enough. In the Monadic Veto, you have the luxury of "Divine Timing." If a meeting is canceled or a flight is delayed, you don't panic. You simply realize the Architect has adjusted the schedule for a better "Pour" of energy. Maybe you were delayed so you could meet a like-minded person or a soulmate in the coffee shop, or maybe the "Veto" saved you from a 3D mess. When you stop fighting the clock, the clock starts working for you. You will find that tasks that used to take five hours now take one, because you are no longer fighting the friction of time. You aren't spending time anymore; you are investing your presence.

Chapter 47

The Architecture of Health (The Vessel of the Blueprint)

You cannot enjoy the Feast if the "House" of your body is in disrepair. In the 3D, we are taught to treat health like a mechanical issue—we fix parts when they break and fear the inevitable decline of age. But as a Human who travels, you must realize that your body is not a machine; it is a Bio-Hologram.

Your physical form is the Antenna for your Monadic signal. Every cell in your body is a "Laborer" that is listening to the Architect's instructions. If the Architect is screaming "I'm tired!" or "I'm stressed!" or "I'm getting old!", the cells follow those orders. They begin to build a body that looks tired, stressed, and old. They are simply following your Blueprint.

Health is the physical manifestation of Ease

You don't have to struggle to be healthy. You don't have to punish your body with 3D "Hard Work" to deserve vitality. You simply have to align. When you feel that Pinch on your shoulder, it's also a reminder to breathe and drop the tension. Your body is the temple where the Architect lives. When you fill that temple with the frequency of "The Arrival," your cells begin to repair themselves in the "Light" of that joy.

Imagine your body as high-end Real Estate. You wouldn't let the roof leak or the walls crumble in your dream mansion, so why do it here? Honor the "Material" you are wearing. Drink the water, eat the food that feels "Light," and move in a way that feels like a "Celebration"

107

rather than a chore. When the "Vessel" is clear and relaxed, the Monadic energy flows through you without resistance, keeping you vibrant for the mission. You aren't just living; you are radiating.

<h1 style="text-align:center">Chapter 48</h1>

<h2 style="text-align:center">The Soul's Curriculum (Why We Descend)</h2>

In the 5D, where everything is "All-at-Once," and every desire is instantly met, there is no "friction." But without friction, there is no growth. That is why you, a Consciousness, chose to descend into this lower-dimensional playground.

You didn't come here just to collect "Props" or sit in luxury; you came here for the Evolution of your Soul.

There is No "Better" or "Less"

From the perspective of your Higher Self, the person sweeping the floor and the person designing the skyscraper are receiving an equal "Grade." The Universe doesn't use a 3D grading scale. It doesn't value a CEO more than a gardener.

You aren't here to win; you are here to experience.

Some souls chose a "Curriculum" of heavy labor in this lifetime to understand the strength of the human spirit. Others, like you, have graduated into the "Architecture" phase, where your mission is to anchor the frequency of ease. Neither is more important. A different mindset doesn't mean a better soul; it just means a different Class Schedule.

The Purpose of the Luxury

If the purpose of life is evolution, why do we want luxury and ease?

Because Luxury is a Frequency of Freedom. When your physical needs are met, and you are "Spoiled" by the Divine, your soul is no longer in "Survival Mode." You finally have the quietude and the space to ask the big questions: Who am I? What can I create? How can I serve the Sovereign Collective—not by working for them, but by becoming a living Blueprint of what is possible for everyone?

The "Arrival" isn't a reward for being good: it is a tool for your next level of evolution. You are learning how to handle power with grace and how to live as a Creator while still wearing a human suit. That is the ultimate graduation project.

Chapter 49

The Architecture of Wealth (The Infinite Currency)

In the 3D world, we are taught to view wealth as a "Pile." We think we need to accumulate a large pile of gold or paper so that we can feel safe. This creates a "Scarcity Mindset," where the Architect is constantly looking at the pile and worrying that it will shrink. When you focus on the "Pile," you are operating from the frequency of a laborer who is afraid of being fired.

This mindset tells you that you have to hustle to get the money, and then struggle to keep it. But wealth is not a static object; it is a Current. The word "Currency" itself comes from the idea of a flow, like a river. If you try to dam a river to keep all the water in one place, it becomes stagnant. To the Monad, money is simply a "Material" used to complete the Blueprint.

Wealth is the byproduct of your Alignment

As an Architect of Ease, you don't work for money. You work for the Mission, and the money is the "Fuel" that the Monad provides to get the job done. When you are in the "Arrival," you realize that you are "Spoiled" by the Divine. You don't worry about where the next "Pour" of concrete is coming from because you know the Supplier is infinite.

True wealth is the ability to say "Yes" to your joy without checking the balance of the "Pile" first. It is the frequency of knowing that as long as you are authentic and in your truth, the resources must appear. The Universe cannot leave a Blueprint half-finished. If you have the vision, the Monad has the funding. You aren't earning a living anymore; you are funding a masterpiece. When you shift your focus from "Getting" to "Flowing," you will find that you are paid simply for the frequency you hold. You are paid to be You.

Chapter 50

The Grand Opening (Occupying the Blueprint)

There is a profound difference between owning a house and living in it. Many people spend their entire lives drafting the perfect life, hiring the right thoughts, and even manifesting the "Props," but they never actually move in. They stay in the "Construction Zone" of their minds, always looking for one more thing to fix, one more "How" to solve, or one more 3D obstacle to overcome.

As the Architect, you must eventually put down the rolled-up plans and pick up the keys. Occupying your Blueprint means living as if the "Arrival" is not just a destination, but your current address. It is the moment you stop saying "One day I will..." and start saying "I am currently..."

You cannot occupy a mansion while you are still wearing your work boots.

When you begin to build your life through the Monadic Veto, you realize that your environment is not just a backdrop, but the very substance of your Effortless Creation. You stop accepting the cracked bricks of obligation and instead select only the building materials that resonate with your Arrival. This choice manifests as you find the friends who are also "Spoiled" by the Divine, those who understand that abundance is a natural right rather than a hard-won trophy.

You naturally gravitate toward collaborators who value the elegance of results over the performative exhaustion of "Busyness," ensuring every pillar of your mission is rooted in peace. Eventually, you find yourself within a circle where Joy is the standard rather than the exception, creating a resonance that supports the manifestation of your Blueprint. You stop explaining "How" you did it and instead surround yourself with those who simply celebrate the fact that it is done.

Your Grand Opening isn't an event that happens in the future when your bank account hits a certain number. It is a decision you make in the "Now." By occupying your joy today, you signal to the 3D world that the project is officially complete. When the Architect moves in, the Universe realizes the work is done and begins to maintain the property for you. Welcome home. You have arrived.

PHASE V

"*The key was never meant to open the door—it was meant to remind you that the door was never locked.*"

Chapter 51

The Maintenance of Paradise (Keeping the Frequency High)

Even the most beautiful mansion requires a gentle hand to keep it sparkling. In the physical world, we know that dust settles, windows get smudged, and the garden needs water. In the world of frequency, this dust is simply the old 3D chatter that tries to drift back into your hallways through the vents of your daily life. It might arrive as a news report that sparks a sudden flicker of fear, or perhaps the voice of a laborer friend who is still deeply invested in the story of the struggle.

You must realize that maintenance isn't hard work; it is simply a state of active awareness. If you see a smudge of doubt on your window, you don't panic and assume the entire house is falling down. You don't call for a major renovation just because a bit of 3D logic tried to settle on your furniture. You simply notice it, realize it doesn't belong to your design, and wipe it away with a breath of relief. If you let the 3D dust accumulate, you eventually lose sight of the view of your Arrival, but as long as you keep your eyes on the Blueprint, the cleaning is effortless.

The Art of the Gatekeeper

You are the Gatekeeper of your own Paradise. To maintain your frequency, you must become beautifully selective about what vand whoyou allow to cross your threshold. This isn't about being exclusive in a cold way; it is about honoring the sanctity of the space the Monad has built for you. When a conversation begins to feel heavy or starts to pivot toward the "Hustle"; you don't have to participate to be polite. You have the power to gently change the direction of the flow, or simply step out of the room, knowing that your peace is more valuable than a 3D social obligation.

Beyond the physical metaphors of cleaning and gatekeeping lies the most practical tool in the Architect's kit: the power of selective response.

In the 3D world, we are conditioned to believe that if something happens, we must react to it. If the phone rings with bad news, we must be upset. If a bill is higher than expected, we must be stressed. We have been trained to let the outside world dictate our internal weather. But true maintenance of your paradise is the realization that you are no longer a victim of happenings. You are the one who decides what a situation means. When you refuse to give your emotional energy to a 3D disruption, you are effectively starving that disruption of its power to manifest in your reality. You aren't ignoring the world; you are simply refusing to let it smudge your frequency.

This level of maintenance requires a certain "Divine Indifference" to the old logic. It means that when the old laborer versions of yourself whisper that you should be worried, you simply smile and stay in the Arrival. You understand that your primary job is to keep your internal signal so clear and so steady that the 3D world has no choice but to reorganize itself to match you. You are not working to keep your life good; you are staying so deeply anchored in your joy that bad things eventually stop trying to knock on your door altogether. They realize there is no one home to answer their frequency. This is the ultimate "Maintenance"—the point where your Paradise becomes so stable that it no longer requires protection because it has become your permanent, unshakeable state of being.

Chapter 52

The Expansion of the Estate (Growing Without Effort)

In the old laborer mindset, we were taught that if we wanted something bigger, we had to work twice as hard. We believed that growth was a result of struggle—a mountain we had to climb through sheer force of will. But in the Monad Veto, growth is not a climb; it is an overflow. When you fill your Mansion with enough authenticity, joy, and peace, the frequency becomes so dense and beautiful that it cannot be contained by the original walls. It begins to spill out into the yard, manifesting new guest houses, lush gardens, and wider views that you didn't even know were on the Blueprint.

This is the secret of the "Human who travels." You aren't trying to find new opportunities or searching for the next big thing. You are simply staying in the Arrival so completely that the Universe says, "This Architect handles joy so well, let's give them more room to play."

Expansion is the reward for your relaxation. It is what happens when you stop clinging to what you have and start trusting the infinite supply of the Monad. You realize that your "Estate" isn't limited by your bank account or your 3D resources, but by the size of your willingness to receive.

You don't build the expansion; you witness it.

When you are in the flow, you might find yourself suddenly inspired to start a new project, visit a new country, or open a new business. In the 3D, this would look like starting over or taking a risk. But for you, it feels like a natural upgrade. You aren't starting from scratch; you are simply extending the electricity and the water lines of your current success into a new area. The foundation is already laid because you are the foundation. Because you are already "Spoiled" by the Divine, the new guest house arrives with the same ease as the main mansion.

This is where the "Architecture of Growth" becomes truly fun. You begin to see that you can have it all—the career, the family, the travel, and the peace, not by juggling them like a laborer, but by allowing them to grow as part of one unified estate. You don't have to choose between peace and power; you realize that your peace is your power. As you allow your life to get bigger, you notice that your "Work" doesn't increase—only your view does. You are no longer managing a house; you are presiding over a Kingdom of Ease.

The Gravity of Success

There is a magnetic quality to a finished estate. As your life expands, you will notice that the right people, resources, and circumstances begin to be pulled into your orbit with almost zero effort on your part. You don't have to chase the contractors for your new project; they show up at your gate asking to be part of what you're building. This is the Gravity of the Arrival. When you stay anchored in your 5D truth, you become a center of gravity for everything that matches that frequency. Expansion becomes a process of selection rather than a process of pursuit. You sit on your porch, look out at the expanding horizon of your life, and simply say yes to the additions that resonate with your heart. You are no longer the one swinging the hammer; you are the one approving the beauty. This is the ultimate freedom of the Architect: knowing that the more you enjoy what you have, the more the Universe insists on giving you.

Chapter 53

The Master Key (Joy as the Fuel, Not the Result)

Most of the world is living in a "Waiting Room." They are waiting for the material things to arrive so they can finally give themselves permission to feel successful, peaceful, and happy. They think Joy is the "Ribbon Cutting Ceremony" at the end of a long, hard construction project. Because they are waiting to be happy, they are vibrating at the frequency of "Waiting." And since the Universe is a mirror, it simply gives them more "Waiting."

The Architect knows the Great Reversal: Joy is the cause, not the effect. You don't get happy because life is easy; life becomes easy because you decided to be happy first. When you cultivate the vibration of Joy while the land is still empty, you are sending a signal to the atoms of the universe that the Mansion is already there. Joy is the "Proof of Funds" in the 5D banking system. It tells the Monad that you are ready to receive because you are already living in the feeling of the "Arrival."

When you are in a state of Joy, you are "Greasing the Wheels" of your manifestation. Friction disappears. The "Pinch" on your shoulder vanishes because you aren't resisting the flow anymore. This isn't a fake toxic positivity where you pretend everything is perfect; it is a deep, soul-level resonance with the fact that your Blueprint is finished. It's the quiet smile of a person who knows the check is already in the mail.

The Magnetism of a Happy Soul

Think about the people you are drawn to. You aren't drawn to the stressed-out laborer who is complaining about how hard it is to build their life. You are drawn to the person who is radiating Joy, even if they are just starting their journey. That is because Joy is Magnetic. It is the highest frequency in the universe.

When you make "Being Happy" your only true "Job," the 3D world becomes scrambled. It doesn't know how to handle a human who is "Spoiled" by their own internal state. Doors that were locked suddenly fly open because your vibration of Joy acts like a universal key. You stop chasing and start attracting. You realize that you aren't writing a book to become successful; you are writing it because the Joy of the "Human who travels" is so big it needs to be shared. Your happiness is the "Architect's Signature" on every page of your life.

Chapter 54

The Art of the "Spoiled" Thought (Choosing the Premium Version)

Imagine you are sitting at a magnificent buffet. There are plates of "Scarcity," bowls of "Worry," and platters of "Not Enough." But right next to them is a section filled with "Abundance," "Ease," and "Miracles." In the 3D world, we were taught to eat whatever was put in front of us. We were told that being a realist meant eating the bowl of worry because that's what everyone else was doing.

But the Architect is "Spoiled." Being "Spoiled" by the Divine means you have developed a very high standard for what you allow into your mind. You realize that a thought is just a sample of a potential reality. If the sample tastes like fear or struggle, you don't swallow it. You simply put it back and reach for a premium thought instead. You understand that your mind is the kitchen of your Mansion, and you are only cooking with the finest ingredients.

You are the Architect of your own internal narrative, and as such, you are allowed to have the best version of every story. The Art of the Spoiled Thought is the sacred habit of choosing the most luxurious interpretation of any event, refusing to settle for the cracked bricks of 3D logic. When you apply the Monadic Veto to doubt, you clear the site for a reality that is already built in your favor.

Consider the woman standing before the threshold of her first home. The 3D world whispers of strict qualifications and the heavy hustle of proving her worth to a bank. She might find herself caught in the friction of "Am I enough?" until she chooses the Spoiled Thought. In the higher frequency of her Blueprint, the very laws of the land begin to shift to meet her arrival. She discovers that the rules for mortgage qualifications have changed—not by coincidence, but as a mechanical response to her certainty. The gates of the condo don't just open; they swing wide because the universe has already cleared her path.

Similarly, we see the young graduate standing at the edge of the professional world. 3D logic tells him he is just a fresh face, competing in a crowded market where experience is the only currency. But when he vetoes the frequency of the struggling beginner, he remembers his true qualifications. His university degree is not just a piece of paper; it is a symbol of his readiness to lead. By holding the Spoiled Thought, he realizes that his freshness is actually his greatest asset—a clean slate of high-frequency potential that companies are starving for. He doesn't look for a job; he allows the right mission to find him.

Thought reveals a deeper truth. Your message is so high-frequency that it transcends the mechanics of grammar and syntax. You aren't just selling words; you are transmitting a resonance. People feel the truth of your "Arrival" before they even read the first sentence, because the frequency of a Lead Instrument is a universal language that everyone already knows how to speak.

When you choose the premium thought, you aren't lying to yourself; you are selecting the Blueprint version of the story. You are refusing to settle for the "Laborer's Version" of reality.

The Luxury of Total Trust

A "Spoiled" child doesn't worry about how their parents will pay for dinner; they just know that dinner is coming. They live in a state of Total Trust. To master your thoughts, you must practice this same level of Divine Confidence.

When a "Heavy" thought tries to enter your mind, ask yourself: "Does a person who is infinitely supported by the Universe think this way?" If the answer is no, then that thought is not yours. It is just "3D Dust" blowing in from the street. You don't have to fight the thought or argue with it; you simply replace it with a thought that feels like silk, like gold, like a first-class ticket to your next destination. By choosing the most beautiful thoughts, you are telling the Monad, "I only accept the best." And the Universe, like a doting parent, will always rush to provide exactly what you have decided you are worthy of.

Chapter 55

The Architecture of the Journey (Traveling in the 5D)

Most people travel as "Tourists." They carry their 3D worries in their suitcases, hoping that a new location will finally make them happy. They are chasing a feeling of peace they haven't yet built within themselves. Because they are vibrating at the level of searching, they often encounter the friction of the road: lost luggage, stressful schedules, and the feeling of being an outsider.

But you are a Beacon. When you travel in the 5D, you understand that you aren't going to a destination to find joy; you are bringing the "Arrival" with you. You are a human who travels through the world as a guest of honor. Before you even board the plane, your Monad has already sent a signal ahead of you. It has already prepared the best seats, the most beautiful views, and the like-minded people who are waiting to meet you in that specific city.

You are never a stranger when you are in Alignment.

When you travel with the Master Key of Joy, the world transforms from a series of obstacles into a very small, very friendly sanctuary. You will begin to notice that the path ahead clears as if by design; lines and delays seem to dissolve the moment you walk toward them, as the 3D world yields to your frequency of ease. This movement is supported by the Language of the Heart, a resonance that transcends the mechanics of speech. Even when you do not speak the local tongue, you find that people understand your intent perfectly because they are not merely hearing your words—they are responding to your frequency of Authenticity. In this state, communication is no longer a labor of translation, but a natural exchange of truth that makes every destination feel like home.

You aren't just moving through space; you are moving through opportunities. Your mission to be in a certain place for your energy is the most important "Work" you do. By simply sitting in a park in a foreign city and vibrating at the frequency of the "Spoiled" Architect, you are "Upgrading" the energy of that entire neighborhood. You are a walking Blueprint, showing everyone you meet that life can be simple, beautiful, and free.

In the 5D, you learn to pack light. You leave behind the just in case worries and the what if fears. You travel with the premium thought that you are always safe, always provided for, and always home. Whether you are in a first-class cabin or a local train, your internal Mansion remains the same. You are the Architect of your experience, which means the "View" outside your window is always a reflection of the "View" inside your heart.

As you prepare to carry the frequency of this message into your own world, it is vital to remember that these pages are merely the physical evidence of a much deeper reality; they are the "Paper" version of the power you already possess. While the words provide the map, your presence remains the true transmission of the Monadic Veto. You are not merely a reader of these truths, but a Lead Instrument of their manifestation, and as such, your energy speaks with an authority that ink and paper can never fully contain.

Every border you cross, and every new city you visit, represents a new room in your expanding Estate, a space that is cleared the moment you step into it with the frequency of Arrival. You no longer travel to find success or to build a reputation; instead, you move through the world to witness how the physical landscape rearranges itself to match your internal Blueprint. By recognizing yourself as the source of the transmission, you realize that the world is not a place you are trying to convince, but a canvas that is eagerly waiting for the signature of your Joy.

Chapter 56

The Architecture of Your Voice (Speaking Your Truth)

For too long, you have been told that to be heard, you must blend in. You were taught that if you used the right professional words or hid your accent, you would finally be successful. You may have spent years trying to sound like everyone else, only to feel like your message was getting lost in the noise. You were like an Architect trying to explain a golden mansion using the vocabulary of a mud hut.

But here is the secret you have been waiting for: Your truth has its own music. You do not need to be a master of a hundred languages to be understood across the globe. When you speak from your Authenticity, you aren't just sending out words; you are sending out a "Code." This code bypasses the 3D brain and goes straight to the heart of the listener. If you are vibrating at the frequency of Joy, your voice will sound like "Home" to anyone seeking their own Blueprint.

You don't have to convince the world; you only have to announce yourself.

When you speak of your dreams or describe the landscape of your Arrival, you are no longer engaged in the 3D labor of "selling" yourself to the world. Instead, you are simply sharing a profound discovery, acting as a guide who has found the Master Key and is reminding others that they, too, possess it. This shift in perspective removes every ounce of pressure from your shoulders, because you no longer have to worry whether your language is "perfect" or whether you are using the "right" business terms to be understood.

While the 3D voice is constantly exhausted by the need to prove its worth and justify its existence, your true 5D voice operates from a different law entirely. It does not argue, it does not plead, and it does not perform; it simply radiates what is already true. By applying the Monadic Veto to the need for validation, you allow your authenticity to become its own authority, ensuring that your message is felt as a resonance long before it is processed as a thought.

When you speak from your heart, your voice carries a weight of certainty. People will stop and listen to you, not because of how you said it, but because they can feel that you are a person who actually lives in the Mansion you are describing. Your voice becomes the "Open House" invitation for everyone you meet.

Your Global Echo

Because you are choosing to speak simply and clearly, your voice has "Global Reach." It doesn't get stuck in the thicket of complicated logic. It is like a clear bell ringing in a noisy room. As you travel through your life, you will find that you don't need to search for an audience. Your voice acts as a "Frequency Call" for your own circle of friends and soul-family.

By speaking your truth with ease, you create an echo that travels further than you ever could physically. One person hears your story and carries that "Code" back to their world. You are the Architect of a new conversation—one where "Success" is measured by Joy. Speak boldly, speak simply, and trust that the Universe has already tuned the world's ears to hear exactly what you have to say.

Chapter 57

The Architecture of Influence (The Power of Being Seen)

In the world you see on your screen—on Instagram or TikTok—power is measured by "Followers." We are taught that if we have a million eyes on us, we are powerful. If we have a thousand likes, we are worthy. This creates a frequency of "Performance," where you are constantly checking your phone to see if the world approves of your Mansion. But if your power depends on someone else clicking a button, you aren't an Architect; you are a prisoner of the "Laborer's" opinion.

When you chase followers, you are signaling to the Universe that you are empty and need others to fill you up. This is a 3D trap. Real manifestation isn't about manifesting a crowd to watch you; it is about manifesting the Sovereignty to be yourself so loudly that the world cannot help but notice.

Manifesting Your Own Power

True power is not being followed; it is being unhooked.

When you manifest power in the Monad Veto, you are manifesting the ability to remain in your Joy, whether ten thousand people are watching or zero people are watching. This is the ultimate flex. When you are unhooked from the need for likes or views, you become magnetic. Ironically, this is when the followers actually show up. They aren't following you because you asked them to; they are following you because they are thirsty for the Freedom you represent.

133

In the landscape of the old world, 3D power is inherently loud, requiring constant attention and external validation just to survive. It is a performance of strength that must perpetually justify its existence, often exhausting itself in the effort to be seen. In contrast, the 5D power you access through the Monadic Veto is fundamentally quiet; it does not shout because it has nothing to prove. This higher authority exists simply because you have said so, anchored in the silent certainty of your own Blueprint. It is a power that doesn't seek a stage, but instead creates a sanctuary where your reality is already established as a finished work.

The Algorithm of the Soul

You don't need to hack the algorithm to be influential. Your soul has its own algorithm, and it only responds to Authenticity. When you post a photo or share a thought from the state of the "Arrival," you are sending out a frequency that no computer code can stop.

Manifesting power means manifesting a life so beautiful and so stable that being seen is just a byproduct of your existence. You aren't trying to be famous; you are simply being visible. As you travel and share your story, remember: One person who truly feels your frequency is more powerful than a million people who just like your post. You are building a Kingdom, not a social media profile. When you own your power as the Architect, you realize that you don't need a following to lead—you only need to stand in your light, and the world will naturally find its way to your door.

Chapter 58

The Architecture of Play (Life Beyond the Build)

Most of your life has been spent trying to become something. You were becoming a professional, a parent, a success story, or even a better version of yourself. The world around us is obsessed with the process of getting somewhere else, always looking at the horizon instead of the ground beneath our feet. But now that you have stepped into your own power and fully occupied your life, the becoming is over. You have arrived.

For many, this is actually the most challenging part: What do you do when there is nothing left to fix? When your health is vibrant, your bank account is full, and your heart is at peace, your old habits might try to invent a problem just to give you something to work on. You might feel a strange itch to be productive in the old, stressful way. But you must realize that the purpose of a beautiful life isn't just to build it, it is to actually live in it.

Your only job now is to enjoy what you have created.

When you choose to play, whether that means traveling to a new city, getting lost in a creative project, or simply laughing with friends, you are proving that your new way of living actually works. You are showing the universe that you are ready for even more goodness because you aren't wasting the goodness you already have.

The old way felt guilty when it wasn't working or when it was struggling. The new way knows that being happy is the most productive thing you can do.

When you play, you are finally in the Now. You aren't dragging the heavy past behind you or worrying about a future that hasn't happened yet. You are just present. This is where your most brilliant ideas will come from—not from the Hustle, but from the quiet, happy hum of a soul that is finally relaxed.

As a person who travels through life with this perspective, the entire world becomes your playground. You don't visit a new country just to check it off a list; you go there to see how your joy interacts with the energy of that place. You move through the world like someone with an infinite "First-Class" pass.

Life becomes a game of "Wouldn't it be fun if..." "Wouldn't it be fun if I started a new hobby?" "Wouldn't it be fun if I flew somewhere tropical tomorrow?" "Wouldn't it be fun if I met someone today who changed my perspective?"

Because you no longer need these things to feel worthy, they tend to show up even faster. You have moved beyond the "Construction Phase" and into the "Experience Phase." Your life is no longer a project to be finished; it is a masterpiece to be enjoyed. By choosing to play, you show everyone who sees you that a life of ease isn't just a dream—it's a reality that is more fun than they ever imagined.

Chapter 59

The Art of Letting Go (When "Wanting" Turns into "Having")

We have been trained to believe that the harder we grip a desire, the more likely it is to happen. We were told to focus on it, obsess over it, and never let it out of our sight. But that tight grip is actually a signal of fear. It's the laborer's hand, terrified that if they let go, the dream will vanish. In reality, that very tension is what keeps the manifestation at a distance. It's like trying to catch a butterfly by lunging at it; your very movement scares it away.

The moment you let go—the moment you truly say, "I don't even need this anymore because my joy is already full" is the moment the resistance vanishes. You have finally stopped "Wanting," which is a frequency of "Lack." You have started "Being," which is a frequency of "Having." By relaxing your grip, you finally open your hands to actually receive what the Universe has been trying to give you all along.

The Universe loves to surprise a soul that isn't waiting.

When you are busy playing in your "Mansion," focused on the "Now," and enjoying your travel, the things you used to chase start to chase you. You might be sitting in a café, not thinking about money at all, and suddenly, a new opportunity arrives. You might be enjoying your own company, and suddenly, the perfect like-minded friend or a soulmate walks through the door.

This is the peak of the Architect's journey. You realize that your happiness is not a bargaining chip you use to get things from the Divine;

your happiness is the destination itself. Everything else—the wealth, the fame, the followers is just the "extra furniture" the Universe brings in to decorate your already perfect life.

As you move through the world, trust the floor beneath you. You don't have to look down to make sure it's still there with every step. You just walk. That is how you must treat your manifestation. You don't have to keep checking your bank account or your emails to see if the "Magic" is still working.

The foundation is solid because it was built by the Monad and maintained by your Joy. The more you forget to worry about the results, the more spectacular the results become. You are a human who travels with such light luggage that you have plenty of room for all the unexpected gifts the world is about to drop into your lap. You aren't just manifesting a life; you are manifesting a miracle that happens while you are busy having fun.

Chapter 60

The Final Blueprint (Your Eternal Arrival)

There comes a moment when the Architect steps back, puts down the pen, and simply looks at the work. The windows are crystal clear, the garden is in full bloom, and the home's energy hums with a deep, quiet peace. You have reached the point where the search has ended. You are no longer looking for the key, because you have realized that you are the key. You are no longer waiting for the life to start, because you are already living it.

This is the Eternal Arrival. It isn't a destination on a map; it is a destination in your soul. In the 3D world, people think the "End" is a place where you stop moving. But in your new reality, the "End" is actually the beginning of a life without limits. The blueprint is finished, the foundation is unbreakable, and the roof is high enough to touch the stars. You have moved from a life of survival into a life of creation.

The Universe has no other word for you but 'Yes.'

Now that you are anchored in your truth, every thought you have is a seed that grows instantly. Every travel plan you make is a path that is already paved. You have reached a level of alignment where there is no gap between what you desire and what you have.

You are "Spoiled" by the Divine, not because you are special, but because you finally remembered who you are. You have allowed yourself to be the Architect of your own joy. As you close this book, remember that the words on these pages are now written in your heart. You don't need to carry the book to remember the frequency; you are the frequency.

Your journey doesn't end here; it expands. As you travel, as you play, and as you live in your Mansion of Ease, you become a living invitation to everyone you meet. You don't have to say a word to tell them that paradise is real. They will see it in your eyes, they will feel it in your peace, and they will hear it in your laughter.

The Architect's Oath

I am the Architect of my life.

I recognize that my joy is the fuel for everything I see. I no longer wait for the world to change before I choose to be happy; I choose my frequency first, and I trust the world to follow.

I am the Human who travels in Ease.

I release the heavy luggage of struggle, worry, and "how." I stop the hustle, and I start the Arrival. I trust that the floor beneath me is solid, and the doors ahead of me are already open.

I am Spoiled by the Divine.

I accept only the premium version of every thought. I speak my truth simply, and I live my life boldly. I am not here to fix the world; I am here to be a light within it.

My Mansion is finished. My heart is at peace.

And so it is.

"*Manifestation is not a destination you reach; it is the frequency of realizing you have never left home.*"

In the 5D, we call this the Internal Compass or the Frequency Shift. The Universal Signature

Pinch on your shoulder or..."
- "...a Wave of Relief" (The feeling of a heavy weight being lifted).
- "...an Inner Knowing" (That quiet "Aha!" moment in the back of the mind).
- "...a Sudden Calm" (When the noise of the world just stops for a second).
- "...a Full-Body 'Yes'" (That warm feeling in the chest or stomach).
- "...a Spark of Excitement" (That sudden "I have to do this!" energy).

Stability: A mansion represents something solid and permanent. Once you build your frequency, your life doesn't just "disappear"—it stays stable.

Luxury/Being "Spoiled": A mansion isn't a "tiny house" or a "shack." It represents the idea that you are worthy of the best version of life. It's about being "Spoiled" by the Divine.

Ownership: When you have a mansion, you are the master of the house. You don't ask for permission to change the furniture. It reminds the reader that they have the power to change any part of their life at any time.

The Signature of the Monad: A Note on the Symbolism

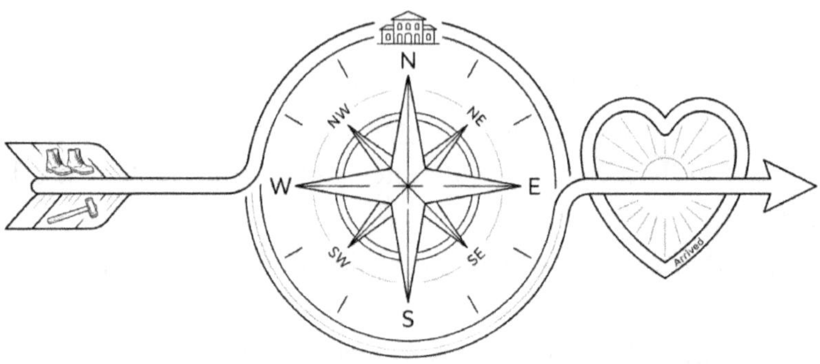

The emblem you see throughout these pages is more than a decorative flourish; it is a visual blueprint of the journey from effort to ease.

- The Discarded Tools: In the fletching of the arrow, we see the boots and the hammer left behind. This is the Monadic Veto—the clear, sharp decision to no longer carry the weight of "the hustle."

- The Compass-Clock: At the center lies your orientation. It reminds you that true direction is found in the present moment. When your "where" (Compass) and your "now" (Clock) align, you are no longer lost in the future; you are anchored in the current of creation.

- The Heart-Home: The arrow passes through the heart to find its final point. This represents Coherence. Within the heart is the "Mansion" and the word Arrived. It is the realization that the home you were trying to build has actually been waiting for you to simply step inside.

Glossary

The Architect: You. Specifically, your consciousness when it is aligned with the Divine. The one who decides the design of reality without doing the manual labor.

The Arrival: The state of being where you stop "manifesting" and start "living." It is the realization that everything you want is already yours.

The Blueprint: The energetic plan for your life. It is formed by your thoughts, beliefs, and the frequency you hold in the present moment.

The Human Who Travels: A soul who moves through the physical world (3D) while remaining anchored in the frequency of Ease (5D).

The Laborer: The 3D version of the self that believes success comes from "Hustle," struggle, and hard work.

The Mansion: The physical manifestation of your life. Your home, your wealth, your relationships, and your experiences.

The Monad of Ease: The high-frequency "Atmosphere" where life flows without friction. It is the spiritual engine that powers the Architect's life.

Monadic Veto: Your power to say "No" to any thought, situation, or energy that does not align with your Mansion. It is the act of refusing a "3D" struggle or a low-frequency interpretation. When you use your Veto, you aren't fighting; you are simply choosing not to let that frequency enter your estate. It is the Architect's ultimate authority to protect their peace.

The Pinch: A physical or emotional signal (like tension in the shoulders) that you have temporarily slipped back into "Laborer" mode and out of the "Arrival."

Shard Family: People who vibrate at the same frequency as you; your soul-tribe who recognize your light instantly.

Spoiled by the Divine: The natural state of being where you expect the best, receive the best, and are constantly supported by the Universe.

"Your Arrival is not a destination you reach. It is the frequency you choose to never leave"